What to Make of Silence

A Collection of Prize-Winning & Favorite Poems

Jane Davis Carpenter

What to Make of Silence
Jane Davis Carpenter

Some poems in this book were written under a generous grant from the Rocky Mountain Women's Institute and were previously published in:

The New York Times
Bloomsbury Review
The Denver Post
Good Housekeeping
Woman's Day
Visions
Salome
Pandora
Blue Unicorn
Collage
The Pen Woman

Other books by Jane Davis Carpenter:
Snapshots
Sightings
Art Nouveau Dreams

Second Advance Edition

Dedicated to
Robert Gardner Carpenter

*Husband and father and cheerleader
for the home teams he adored,
including his own.*

Contents

Introduction

Poetinkering

Were it not for deadlines, many of these poems would never have been finished.

So reluctant am I to let them go (to a contest, to a publisher) because I am always certain that more work would perfect them: just a little tweaking here and there, tinkering like a mechanic listening for a certain sound from an engine.

That this sound evades the mechanic is parallel to my own craft. Once in a great while, a poem hums. When it happens that way, it's been in my head for days before I seat my questing self at the keyboard. My task is 'caging the wild words' so as to make prior effort invisible, to serve long-wrought verse up as if fresh-minted.

You will find here the substance of six decades of living, observing, distilling. Thank you for opening the covers of my book. I hope your curiosity and your courage are both rewarded.

Jane Davis Carpenter
Denver, 2009

What to Make of Silence

We can almost see it, as if it were
The ghost of earlier dialogues.
It shimmers a little, silvery in
The midst of night shadows.

This house is an old house;
In a high wind it creaks as
If an ancient sailing ship
Seeking safe harbor. Of
Safe harbors there are few,
But their silence is deep.

Far off is the silver ring
Of the buoys, the cries of
Free-wheeling gulls aloft.
Without the silence,
We would hear none of
These. The crash of waves
Against the rocks, that too
Would be remembered, not
Heard while happening.

What to make of silence?
Meditation, to begin with;
Time that seems infinite
But that cannot contain all,
Everything being equal.

Cast-on stitches on a needle;
Cast-off, outmoded designs
Willingly give up their place.

If you used a swan-quill
You could hear a letter
Being written; there are
Scratchings on the surface
Of the paper – pay them heed.

Love and Other Dangerous Emotions

Without any risk, where's the fun...

Love in a Loaf of Fresh-Baked Bread

The scent of cinnamon's magnetic force,
The yeastiness of baking bread unmatched
For pure allure: all steps lead to the source
On Homecoming, as soon as door's unlatched.
The kitchen is a gathering-place for love,
Each act of nurturing a testament.
A random reach in cookie jar will prove
Your favorites are there, and circumvent
All notions of your lack of self-esteem.
The one who loves you best baked all of these:
To show your world less harsh than it might seem;
To find warmth there, and comfort, and heart's ease.

Is love life's leaven, causing it to rise?
Do you doubt what you see with your own eyes?

Recycled Valentine

Here is my heart:
It's been around
The block a time
Or two, tattered
Paper lace like
Band-Aids hiding
The worst inflicted
Injuries. Tangles of
Ribbon make a maze
Of my secret history.
Pray do not notice
Plops and splotches
From long-ago tears
The source of which
Matters not, not now.
You, my very dear,
Will mend this heart
And make all hope
Renew itself. (again)

Disclaimer

The following poem contains material that some readers may find hopelessly romantic. Reader discretion advised.

I never meant to fall in love again.
God knows, it was quite bad enough when young!
The weeks of wondering how, and where and when—
Our reputations by a thread were hung.

Remember walking in the rain in Spring?
And trellised roses climbing up a wall?
Remember thinking we, tone-deaf, could sing?
Such dizzy heights! Far greater was our fall. . .

For all such loss, I cannot help but grieve,
Though life is simpler now, more circumspect—
I never meant to be the first to leave,
Now all I have left is my self-respect.

But pride is little comfort to the proud!
I wish I'd known how much more was allowed.

No Trumpets

I thought there would be trumpets when we met,
And cymbals crashing like a thunderstorm
When we, at long last, found each other's lips.

I wondered at the time if Cupid had
Miscued us both. There we were, caught by rain,
Entranced too deep for seeking shelter yet,
Warmed by our own small inner fire, amazed
At how compelling kisses are, when right.

Too soon, we had to go back to our friends,
Whose lamplit windows we could see from where
We were – but suddenly too shy to share.

You took your own coat off, wet though it was,
And tented it above our heedless heads.
We laughed; it was belated chivalry,
But still – I did not miss the trumpets then
And never have, in all the years between.

Distances

Because I do not know,
Because I do not want to know
How far it is from where I am
To where you are,
I play myself a game.
A small, evasive kind of game:
The rules are mine—always the same:
How far to where you are?
Just hours by air
(And hundreds of nonexistent dollars),
If I got on an Eastbound plane,
If Life would play my game.
Because I do not care to know,
How many minutes it may pace
Of talk on rented wires,
Outflow from you and me.
Because I do not know,
Because I do not need to know
How far it is from where I am
To where you are—
It is as long as a deep sigh.

Dia de los Muertos

Remembering an old love.

You wandered into my heart
So recklessly, not at all sure
Of your welcome—who could
Resist that show of courage?

This was no fairytale fantasy:
No dragons to slay, no moat
To cross—just a virginal heart
Sounding like distant drumbeats,
As if it might escape my chest.

Escape there was none, not for us.
Our lives were braided together
From the moment of impact on.

Everyone else thinks you're gone,
Gone these dozen years—but no
One knows you visit me still:
When my defenses are down,
In that instant just before sleep
When dreams are all we have
As levees against the daily storm.

I tell you only this: You wandered
Into my heart and never really left.

Seven A.M.

My darling, from the deep
Scuba-land of sleep
You seem regretfully to surface.
What trophy do you bear
Back to the deck-flat everyday?
You seem now fretfully
To speak
But words are still aqueous.
One hand clutches,
Other wards away
And no one could say
If you protect
What you have
Or else reject
What you love,
But dare not keep.
There are wrecks down there, down deep,
Of dreams, your own and others' sleep.

At Breakfast 1

Tell me, tell me where you were
Last night, while we lay sleeping.
Your face still wears that dream
You're so afraid to confess to—
Its shadows sculpt your bones.
And still you shrug and say,
"I never dream, or can't recall
It if I do." Tell me, is this true?

Tell me, tell me what you saw
Last night in your mind's eye—
Since your day's eye was shut,
Tell me everything you saw.

At Breakfast 2

I see you reach across the table,
Not for toast, or jam to put on it,
But for the Spring Seed Catalog,
The most hopeful harbinger
In our small and private world.

"I was dreaming," you begin,
But alter it to "thinking"
From some notion of manliness,
"Thinking how we could keep
A salad garden going this year.
You'd like that, wouldn't you?"

My smile is answer enough.
Rationally, I know nothing
We have ever tried to grow
Remotely resembles the photos
In the catalog, artfully juiced
Up in amazing spread of color.
Watch how they work their
Always-seductive, subtle magic.

And a man who insists he
Is not a dreamer is possessed
Perennially by a reason
To hope once more, I think—
But I keep it to myself. He must
Not know that I know! Some
Things are inviolate in our
Small and private world.

Hands

Hands folded beseech,
But they cannot hold;
Hands open can reach
And be blessed tenfold.

The pure art of loving is easy to learn—
Hold close with hands open and love will return.

Hands held like a cup
Can capture the rain
For thirst to drink up
And be filled again.

So endless God's love, why should we know greed?
To each shall be given according to need.

Hands touch and revive;
Tend babies; bake bread;
Make music of life,
Where love's always led.

Little Nocturne

The moon is falling low.

Unlace your fingers from my hair,
And lift your cheek from mine,
And let your feet persuade you to the door.
But, if you can do none of these,
Then slip your arms about me this once more,
Because you are not even gone before
I miss you more than I can bear.

The moon will rise again.

Love Letter to a Muse

You are the water;
I am your cup.
Chained to a pump,
My dented tin shape
Holds the coldest
Water from the well.
It's like no other
Anywhere. Fresh,
So cold it takes away
The dust of Summer
And too many roads
Travelled too many times.

You are the wine;
I am the crystal flute
Waiting for you to swirl
Me like a dancer once
Again. I have waited
For you as long as I can;
Now I am impelled
To move, to make words
Form a new song, sung
In a way I can love
As much as I have learned
To fear and to love you.

Fill me.

Love Song for an Old Love

When all the words are spoken
And all the songs are sung,
I vow I will remember
The time when we were young.

The golden sands of seashore,
The silver stars of night,
And waking up each morning
To every new delight.

The world was very old then,
A host had loved before;
We thought ourselves the first pair
To knock upon that door.

What we did NOT know blessed us;
We learned reluctantly
And tasted in our Eden
The fruit of that first tree.

When I am old, remember
My face as I was then,
As yours I always treasure,
My true love and my friend.

When all the words are spoken,
And all the songs are sung,
We know there is no splendor
Like that when we were young.

Variations on a Theme by Dante

There is no greater pain than to recall a happy time in wretchedness,
-Dante Alighieri

I shall return one day, when you have lost
The dream for which you search most ardently;
When, in Spring, soft-fingered rain shall most
Insistently provoke your heart to memory;
Or, at the last leaf's falling, you will sigh,
And suddenly feel aged, while still young,
And seek an answer, but find no reply:
I am the song you once believed was sung.

Notes on a Rainy Night in Spring

What matters is: Not lightning, thunder, or
The hovering cloud above the distant hills—
What matters is, I think, the scent of rain
When everything so longs to bloom anew.

When, finally, the rain comes, curtain-like,
A new show's staged—it's almost magical.
The stage directions read: "Go for a stroll."

No better time to walk on country lanes,
When lilac-fragrance meets the smell of loam
Made sharper by the touch of Springtime rain.

Our memories are filled with rainy walks,
Strolls taken for discoveries of love,
Or ways to ward off love's acute despair.

On city streets, reflections neon-bright
May shimmer on wet pavements as you walk.
And street musicians syncopate the night:
A bitter blues goes well with tears of rain.

Colorado Boulevard, Late on a Rainy Saturday Night

The old "Chicago"bard
With his shock of hair
Like cornsilk falling
Over his Norse-blue eyes
And his shock of language
(don't forget how tough he had to be)
Nevertheless became soft
And sentimental about
— of all things! —
Downtown traffic lights
Seen from a homing plane.

He opined his City looked
Like an emerald and ruby necklace
Displayed on a black velvet
Jeweler's cloth.
Though one assumes
Of Sandburg he knew little
Of jeweler's showrooms
And cared even less about
Ladies who wore their gems
Instead of hocking them and
Feeding a thousand of the poor.

Dear Carl, I need you at this
Hopeless hour! My boulevard
Wears cheap and gaudy finery
Made out of varicolored neon
And, what's more, I'm sure
　　the
　　　gems
　　　　are
　　　　　only
　　　　　　glass.

Weather

That day, that special day that will never come again...

Still Life

The pearly sheen of fruit set on the windowsill,
Round cheek of apple; curve of pear, turned toward the sun,
Reminds of old Dutch paintings.

Look! How the dust-motes dance in the bright shaft;
See! How the curtains billow softly in the breeze;
Listen! To the birdsong filtered through the hush of sleepy noon.

All this is happening upon a certain Summer's day,
The one that just precedes the Fall's first frost—
The one that, yearly, takes us by surprise.
Unfairly, we, who should remember other Autumns, fail:
The natural progression find once more too quick.

Our consolation is:
This is the moment when that fruit
Is ripe and ready.
We have watched, and seen, and listened.

Are we ready now to taste?

The Harbingers

If, in our youth, we always wished for Spring,
To see May flowers into arbors formed,
To hear the birds' sweet-voiced remembering;
To touch safe harbor when the seas have stormed,
Then must we grow, mature, and graduate
From universities of life well-taught;
Succeed, unwillingly, to this estate;
We may not, by mid-life, find what we sought.
To recognize our limitations' bounds
Becomes a measure of our growth so far.
If we are luckier still, a cheer resounds
As one of us becomes a shooting star.
At last, the harbingers of change may sing,
Forgetting naught, remembering everything!

In Autumn

This stateliness no stranger to me now,
The path I take both decorous and safe,
I dance again (my heart remembers how)
If dignity should bind too tight or chafe.
I love this season: its defiant pace
Which matches mine, somewhat, and for its leaves
Afire with color one last time, to race
The coming of first frost my heart believes
Will never be. My heart believes the lies
It likes, unhampered by a need for fact!
From love's equations, the heart multiplies;
From experience, it must subtract.

The heart remembers differently, I find,
From all the convolutions of the mind.

'Round Midnight

The snow stealthed in,
Heavy, wet, clinging,
Leaving behind this:
Landscape of broken
Boughs, scars on bark,
Trees of sturdy girth
Diminished by loss.

Most ominous of all,
A downed bough leans
Against the house, too
Heavy to move by hand
Even for these arborists
Who look like loggers.

The lesser limbs spread
Out among the others,
Are delicate as harpstrings
Through which a phantom
Melody seems to rise.

The machines arrive, man
Made twelve times stronger,
And hoist the biggest bough,
Chipping it into sawdust as
A *coup de grace*. Then all
The errant fallen limbs are
Gathered into a bundle like
A nosegay for King Kong
And order is restored to
The violated front lawn.

Silhouettes of newly pruned
Maples, Norway and Silver
Leaf, reach skyward. What
Is left of them is spirit, pure
Stubborn spirit, and new shapes
For them to learn to grow into.

Storm Warnings

My vulnerable bones suddenly seem venerable as well.
When a storm's moving in, the joints' aches sharpen
And I feel like a caricature of an aging woman, saying
Like an ancient sibyl, "Snow by morning." So I don't say it,
But all the same, morning brings ice crystals on windowpanes,
Snow swirling as if it means it. Beautiful, relentless it falls.

There is no storm in my body, I rejoice to discover on waking.
No fevers making the bones shake. A hymn of praise for Ceres
For making the good grain grow rises to my lips which seek
Coffee and other creature comforts. Snow seems to purify,
To make my motives blameless—even if they are not.
Most especially, perhaps, if they are not.

Storm warnings can sometimes be revoked.
Let the bones warm awhile in the sun and see
How it all may just possibly work out.

The Wing Chair

This is her place for reading,
Bowl of Gala apples nearby,
Pen and paper at the ready—
She likes to argue with authors
But will not mar a book's page
With impulsive marginalia.

This is her place for dreaming;
The wing chair has pretentions;
It is not enough to shield from
Drafts, but it assumes an angel
Guise (must be the wings?) and
That may be cause for alarm.

This is her place for restoring,
Recalling the warm lamplight
In her grandmother's kitchen,
A kerosene lantern replaced
Now by halogen bulb in brass—
Brighter, but not to say better.

A Winter storm howls outside,
Seeming determined to get in.
She pays it very little mind;
Her eyes are on these pages
Her hands caress with love,
Vellum vs. wind velocity.

Night Visitors

The house has lived here
For a century,
At night so like the hulls
Of ancient sailing ships,
Wooden timbers creaking
In wind and weather shifts,
Revealing voices like
Those of night visitors,
As if from a crow's nest
Or unseen pilot at the helm.

If I were a figurehead upon
My prow, searching shoals
For dangers yet unknown,
What would I feel, indeed,
If I found such, and who
Would I have to warn?
Myself, perhaps, for
Setting sail at night
On what might turn
A storm-tossed sea?

I seek safe harbor
When I go to sleep
And, so far, I have
Found it there: Bed
Is not at risk for me
Who am all the crew
There is for my vessel.
Still, a seaman's prayer
Would not go amiss,
Reminding all my saints
That my ship is small
Upon a vast, uncertain sea.

Wind Rising

All this late-Autumn day
The wind has rattled shutters,
Blown the last, stubborn leaves
From off our trees, and now it
Comes to this: howling lest
It be dismissed as mere weather.

This is not weather; sounds like
These howls come from coyotes'
Throats, or big cats' lately here
From their mountain lairs to try
Their luck with people as prey.

It subsides enough to be those two
Eternally doomed lovers still there
On the moors, calling to each other.
The sound becomes as moaning under
The eaves, "Let me in! Let me in!"

By morning, some kind of order is
Restored to your world. It was only,
After all, weather, and you unafraid.

The Winter Beach

Last Summer was another country, a place
Where small events were never trivial,
Where larger ones were not allowed in:
Newspapers with ominous headlines
Were a long walk to the general store
Away, so days went by when we knew nothing
Of the great outside world; our private universe
Was here, where finding a nautilus shell
Miraculously intact: news to be shared.

Now, in November, even the air has a
Sharper tooth, the salt upon the tongue
Is savored for its bite. Wind eddies up
Sand upon the orange fences against snow,
Against losing any more land to the sea.

Wind behind the sand makes little needles
Of the grains to prick the face awake again;
Watch where you place your feet, if you
Would walk close to the ruffled edge of
Storm-stirred water. Go on, finish your walk
Knowing when you return to the beach cottage
A crackling hearth will welcome you back.

It's that thought that makes possible this walk:
Remembered pleasures like hot tea in a mug,
A hug warm as his woolen sweater is wide,
Feet to the fireplace fender, soles and soul
Both coaxed back, recalling how it was
To be so cold, and now warmed to the heart.

Family Favorites

*Smile indulgently, but never forget
the importance of kinship...*

Prologue: Tell Me Something About Yourself

When my hair was cornsilk tassels
Down my back, disciplined to
Pigtails, and all the world
A big electric storm (not far,
Yet not too close; everything
Was loud enough to hear and bright
Enough to see) say, five miles away;
My mind was patterned like a piece of chintz,
Flower-shapes cluttering every inch of it,
And brighter where no light
Had touched to fade them, hid in folds
Where eight-year-old imagination holds
The best, most wonderful of secrets,
Secrets that were never really true.

There was a gnarled old lady of an apple tree
In my back yard, pretty only in the Spring
With blossoming, but friendly always,
And smelling of sun on just-washed clothes.
There was an oak I trusted with my swing.
A dignified old deacon, was this oak;

It was like sitting in his lap for stories
To pump my swing and hear the whispers
Of the leaves in amiable reply to breezes
A chance gust blew there; the big puffs
Of wind broke into fragmentary pieces
When they met the hard oldness of this oak.

I was not allowed to stand beneath the trees
If a storm should suddenly come close,
And I always ran for the house slowly as I could,
Feeling the worst deserter; waiting for the wood
To splinter from a lightning bolt that never came.

There was in the house that raised me
A cookie jar on the middle pantry shelf.
It kept its secrets well and nobody,
I was powerfully convinced, could tell
How many cookies went into a pocket after school—
They were such a spicy heap and surely, all uncounted,
So familiar they were hardly seen,
So deeply known as not to be forgotten now.

Tell me something about yourself.
Tell this person about the pantry shelf;
The swing hung from the patriarchal oak;
About the motion and the taste
Of a certain place, of a certain time?
It is impossible that one would know the place,
Or even just its name.

New

The birthing room is pink
In early morning light;
Sunlit shafts of hope
Bless the bed where lie
Mother and infant, baby
Curled up like the shell
Shape he was when he began.

Gone are the shadows
Of the night, terrors
Shapeless but ombering
Every corner of this room.
False cheer did not light
The corners ("What could
Happen?" Answer: *Anything...)*

Now that morning is here,
And mother and baby here,
Safe and warm and alive—
NOW is the time to rejoice.
("What happened?" EVERYTHING!)

Hospital Scene

Encapsuled in this green and glassy room
Where terror flowers like chrysanthemums
In silence, waiting attitudes become
More like a gardener's, linking his green thumbs
And, incidentally, his hands in prayer.

This woman, in apostrophe of grief,
Might be assessing aphids' damage where
She fiercely looks upon the rose's leaf;
That tall and hollowed man might be aware
Of hummingbirds that beat on Summer air,
Another time, another place, not now.

Just now, he is mere mortal in his hour
Of doubting immortality. For how
Can he forget the fearsome year no bower
Graced his gate, or when the iris failed?
Though he believed in one eternal spring
Pictorial visions of his garden failed.

He is undone by his remembering
The trophies in the catalog unmimed
Successfully in his small plot of earth.

The doctors, after all, took X-rays, timed
Her operation; charted life from birth—
They know her body better than he does.

And yet—they've never seen her special smile,
The one she saves for him; whatever was,
Or yet may be, he cultivates that smile.

Polaroid Instant

On a blue-domed, late-summer day,
We are being sea-creatures, beached
By green-glass, crashing waves.

Our daughter, sea-nymph for now,
Is brushing sand and salt
From out her long, sun-streaked hair,
Sand- and salt-covered silken strata.

Her father stealthily picks up camera
To capture the naiad no net can catch.
In that Polaroid instant, I cast back
My net of memory and superimpose another
Image over hers: myself at 14, and it matches!

Somewhere, under this slim, well-oiled machine
Of a well-preserved woman there remains a girl.
I announce recklessly to our fetching nymph,
Who knows no need of subterfuge or subtleties,
"I'll race you down to the ice-cream stand!"

Pray for me, all you baskers in the sun,
All you watchers of the sea;
I need this tiny victory.

To My Child, Learning to Read

Dear Betsy, open your old picture book:
You see that scarlet bird among the boughs?
Once, long ago, you could but mutely look,
Admire, and never risk the scholar's vows
You take with your first sight-read word, to know
What kind of bird is shown, and where he lives,
And can he bear to flame against the snow
An artist's contrast in this picture gives?
Is he a tanager or cardinal?
Who feeds him when he shivers with the cold?
He is so small to be so beautiful;
You read until his story is all told.

A little world of things has just occurred
Since you began to read about your bird.

To My Daughter, Away on Her Birthday

If I could somehow give you everything you dream.
I'd grant you mountain boots to hike beside a stream;
Your backpack would stow: fruit and cheese and bread, white
wine;
Spring water for canteen, and traveler's prayers of mine.

The weather where you are is steady, stubborn rain—
I'd send you bright-blue summer days till you returned again,
And thick pines for a shade when you would stop to rest,
And one small dove of purest white to be your mealtime guest.

But fancies are not biddable, to wrap and mail,
Some awkward shapes and sizes; some, awesomely frail—
I send instead this chained heart of silver wrought
And a small sum of money for what *can* be bought.

A Look at the Family Album

At twenty-two or so, my mother wore
The face of a rather knowing angel,
The faintest of lines beginning to appear,
Mouth's curve is half-seraphic,
Half-sophisticate;
Her tawny hair is
Back-lit soft to halo
That nearly-serene brow.
Her hands are folded like large lilies,
Thus telling little lies
About their capabilities.
This seeming seraph
Carried a canoe overland
And pitched a tent, and built a fire, and cooked,
And never once said she would rather be
Exploring concrete canyons in her own city.
She cleaned the fish my father caught,
Wrinkling her nose, but not
Refusing a gift from the stream,
Wrapped in sweet meadow-grass,
For breakfast...
And the day had just begun.

Elizabeth at Seventeen

Renoir the painter would have loved her,
Sitting in that golden light:
Montage of pinks and blues—a mauve blur
Rounds her cheek and charms the sight.
(Her grandmother cherishes this picture.)

The dusky time of day in Autumn
Shared with boys from football fields,
Is dazzling still to her who caught him,
He whose smile the charm reveals
(The yearbook can't do justice to this picture.)

On any day at breakfast greetings,
Gaily gilded shining head
Takes precedence. The dull, known meetings
Dim beside what she's just said.
(Her parents try to hold this picture.)

Her cat, the warm and furry charmer,
Purrs his happiness with her:
The contrast of gold hair, black fur
Makes a silhouette together.
(The cat's the only patient creature.)

The Potter Is My Daughter

This tall room, her studio, is grey
With antique dust of classic clay—
The same, the same, as centuries
Ago was frozen in a frieze.
The same, the same, as Grecian urn
Fired in the kiln on some Aegean shore
For some to venture, some to learn
The clay is strata of Hellenic lore.
Her small and certain hands grow strong, when pulled
Against the whirring of her potter's wheel.
The legends, legion, she's been told
Have given her a sure, surprising feel:
What shapes await her eyes' discovery,
Needing this potter's hand to set them free?

Family Reunion

Long picnic tables, silvery as barnwood, fill
The grape arbor,
Like ships in a harbor:
A reunion regatta.

They're freighted down with such a Summerful
Cargo of primary-
Color foods, culinary
Fugue and toccata...

Such medleys of fruits and cheese and spices,
Such melodies of color, grape to peach!
The grandmothers, the mothers, hope it suffices,
Leaves every celebrant too sated, far, for speech.

"Don't you TOUCH that!" rings out with authority;
A small hand creeps
Back from cornucopia heaps
Of food to table's thin edge.

One table alone holds a dozen kinds of pastry:
Oozing with juice
Of Summer's fruits;
Small hand sneaks a slim wedge.

Babies tumble like a litter of round kittens,
Near the feet of their
Preoccupied mothers,
Make exploratory mews.

"Now tell about the table where the salad glistens."
Sprigged with parsley,
Dressed with oil, shiny
In the green cool.

Some sparkle with ripe fruit in gelatins;
Some are shaped, are ringed or welled or mounded;
Some return to where the families begin;
Their origins are sure to be expounded.

Under a net canopy, crowned with pineapple rings,
Reigns the handsomest ham,
Reason enough for some aunt's fame;
It's fragrant with rehydrated love.

The round and rosy ladies of three motherings
Frankly share their best,
Wanting all the rest
To taste their life, and find it good.

Remember, <u>remember</u>, say sisters to each other;
Remember, remember, calls cousin to cousin.
Remarks one favorite aunt, "You look <u>just</u> like your
mother!"
We smile in concord: "That's what we've BECOME."

To My Father

My father was a gentle man whose heart stopped when too
full:
He saw our nation's Bicentennial, and raised a cheer,
As all old soldiers, disciplined to Parade Rest, will.
He hung on gallantly, determined to salute that year.
He waved a tiny Flag; his eyes were wet with weary tears,
He drank a dram of sherry as a toast, and sighed, and slept;
But hours later, his blue eyes had blazed at all his dears,
Around his bedside in review-we *could not* then have wept.
He was a soldier to the last, and we could but salute
That gentle heart, that soldier's foot, that no more could
wear boot.
My mother tells a legend that the last word Father spoke
Was "Hip-hip-hooray!" She never felt it when her poor heart
broke.

My Mother Telescopes Her Household

There are left here only the most loved
Of all possessions fifty years amass;
She knows full well they cannot all be moved—
She must make choices, as she often has.
She has condensed from big house to small, too,
She joked: not even attic room for mice—
Now she condensed four rooms into two
With barrels from the house before
Moved and left unopened; she must have missed
Her favorite things and yearned to bring them out:
In tarnish-proof wraps, is the silver kissed
With shine? Does Persian carpet glow without
The magic touch of light, when carpet's rolled?
The tiny, fluted coffee cups are packed
In shredded, yellowed newspapers, so old
Their stories are like history, intact.
Are they still charming, seen ten years from now?
These were a very major pleasure, then.
Subdued by being exiled to endow
The lucky children, and the grandchildren
Who live a differing way from hers, today.
My mother dials her phone, and calls to me:
"Do you want these things? Can you, possibly?"
When I was small, I asked: *"What will become
Of all your pretty things, when I am wed?"*
It was complex as a chrysanthemum
Bloomed to a shaggy, multipetaled head.
Sure of my dowry as of wedding rings,
My mother told me, *"Do not dwell on things—
Possessions make your life a sweet morass."*
Grandmother said, *"Be careful what you wish;
You may be granted, too soon, what you ask."*
And now I have my dream, to the last dish!

A Visit with My Aunt

Sing me a song of faraway lands;
Tell me of bygone times!
Let me hold history here in my hands;
Spin me a yarn that limns
Each generation's telling anew
What you remember now.
Tales your own teachers re-told to you,
Reaching for "WHY?" and "HOW?"
When did my people set out to roam?
Why did they settle here?
How did they know when they had come home?
What did they pioneer?
Proud as I am to hear of their deeds
(Braver, by far, than mine),
Each is a candle, lit for my needs,
Hallowed by history's shrine.

Time Frozen: Family Album

Their image shimmering on the air,
Together, in a too-big chair,
My daughter and a sleepy cat
Still occupy the place they sat
To catch the winter's lemon sun
When she was five, and he was one.

They waited somnolent, the two,
For someone passing, someone who
Had hugs to spare, or pats for cats.

Since then, of course, their thermostats
Predict a harsher weather now!
They ask for what life will allow.

Braiding Betsy's Hair

Present, past and future here
Twine themselves as one—
Brushing, braiding Betsy's hair
In the morning sun.
This is magic time for us,
Braiding close our lives:
As I stroke with rhythmic brush,
Time long gone revives
And renews our bond once more:
Child who sits and hears;
Mother needing to explore
Past and future years.

Water Baby

For my grandson, a brand-new Aquarian.

Hands like smallest starfish;
On fingers, tiny shells;
Skin luminous
As phosphorus
From sudden ocean swells,
Your voyage here a wish
Fulfilled as promise kept;
Your terra-world has whirled
While you have slept.

Reflections in a Mirror of the Past

Long after the smudges of small fingerprints
Have all been polished out of existence,
And toys mysteriously strewn all over
The just cleaned, party-perfect house,
And wilting bouquets of prize flowers
With snapped-off stems were left for you,
And cakes for the church bake sale
Were nibbled at, leaving telltale crumbs –
You look around your quiet, tidy house
And wish with all your heart to have
Such sweet disorder restored to you again.

First Birthday

For my grandson.

First time we met, you were minutes old,
Just out of your snug nine months' home, and cold,
Perhaps, and angry, bellowing and red—
And wanting to be held, and soothed, and fed.
Now you are twelve months hatched, and I could swear
No other baby can to you compare:
You ran before you even tried to walk;
You make real conversation when you talk;
You seem, though we are many sleeps apart,
To welcome me again with your whole heart.
Before you came, I vowed I'd never be
A braggart grandma—but now look at me!

Cradle Song

My mother made her needle sing
A cradle song, and stayed up half the night
The eve of her first grandchild's christening,
She stitched a dozen tucks, and filigreed
With lace a doll-sized petticoat
No eyes but hers and mine (and God's, of course)
Would, likely, ever see.
I teased her gently, coaxed her off to bed,
And praised her wondrous work, as well I could:
It was a fairy wing, so gossamer,
Yet spotted with one ruby dot of blood—
For human fingers, pricked, must always bleed.
A hundred times, the silvery needle flashed,
And, on the last, the testament of truth:
Mortality with fairy legend clashed.
I stayed up one brief moment more
To wash the linen fair as it had been before—
Unwilling to concede catastrophe,
Though miniature, might mar this memory.

My Mother Makes a Party

Enter the shining room, bright with excitement now,
Burnished with polish,
Arbored with flowers, all the candles lit.
Treasure these hours:
There will be talk, and good food, and music here—
You make the party,
You are the presence, so you are made to feel—
All that was lacking
To make this afternoon or evening real.
Nothing is mentioned
Of all the hours spent weaving the magical
Ambience abounding:
Ironing a banquet-sized pale damask tablecloth,
Shining the tea set,
Washing best crystal in water so hot it scalds,
Planning the menu:
Chopping and slicing, creaming and cooking all,
Making ambrosia
Fit (of course) for all the gods of Olympus,
Lest you had wondered,
Ever, your worth:
You are Olympian in all save birth,
Once inside my mother's door—
Her party makes you feel far nobler than you did before.

Villanelle for My Mother

Ida Norman Davis, 1896-1990

The seasons turn in their elusive way,
And sometimes it is easy to forget:
The sun, the sea, the gulls, that final day.

We walked with you along a stony quay,
You who would not allow us to regret
How seasons turn in their elusive way.

Our benison, a kiss from ocean spray
Reminded us of our most lasting debt,
The sun, the sea, the gulls, that final day.

Remember how we sailed around the bay:
The sun's late warmth still lingering, and yet
The seasons foreordained to turn that day?

Upon the waters, we cast our bouquet
Of memories to last beyond sunset.
The seasons turn in their elusive way,
But sun and sea were ours, that final day.

Second Spring

I would have gathered all my garden's flowers,
Still gemmed at dawn with little pearls of dew,
If they could possibly enhance the hours
Of lifetimes shared, of love-times spent with you-
But spent so recklessly! As if we could
Imagine all our wealth would last for years!
I tell you this: I always thought your good
Was strong enough to overcome my fears;
That there was nothing that could not be bought
With pledges and tokens, I confess –
That we would find what we had always sought –
The odds a gambler would not even guess!

This is the second Spring since you are gone,
My garden flowers *still* as fresh as dawn.

Old Collegiate Air at Reunion

Of marble frieze
And Gothic spire
For being hauntingly a history;
Of classic lyre
For being tauntingly a mystery ---
Who would admit
Where now we sit
The wrong of these?

The pattern shaped
All contours small.
These reachings toward remembrance are endured;
Politely, all
The names of those who failed are now obscured:
Some walk alone,
Some we have known,
Some life has raped.

The rhythm's strummed;
Refrain is hummed,
The beat tormenting to a dancer's feet
The answers plumbed
Where palest ashes of the past are sweet
To urgent tongue,
Are praised and sung;
Refrain is hummed.

Itinerary

Your smile that breaks so gently through your face,
Beginning in your eyes and traveling down
To curve your cheek more sweetly than before,
Enclose your mouth in deep parentheses,
And tilt your chin up quizzically, will reach
Its destination when it finds my heart.
This is a journey—though I know it well—
I never tire of charting yet again.

School Shoes

I felt like Cinderella's ugliest stepsister,
Trying to cram my toes into a size smaller
Than I could wear, at 12, after Summer
Going barefoot or in flipflops or sneakers.
The unthinkable had happened again—
I was going to be a giantess, it was certain.

Perhaps I could wear floppy clown shoes
And make small children giggle, if not
Inspire pining sonnets from boys unmet
As yet—but I knew they were out there.
I was just waiting for them to notice me.

Who would not notice a 12-year-old with
Unfulfilled shape, wearing such huge shoes?
It wouldn't matter how I dressed or wore
My cornsilk hair or if I knew football stats.
I had seen puppies with outsized paws ,
The ones you knew would be Great Danes.

I would be a Great Girl, that's all, far bigger
Than my elegant mother for whose sake
Doors were held and chairs placed just so.

"Let her open her own doors! God knows,
She's certainly BIG enough!" they'd say.
All those avuncular pats on the head, all those
Welcome words about my blue, blue eyes
Would disappear, every one. "I was rather
Cute as a kid," I'd console myself at twelve.
"A quality that's greatly overrated," I'd add.
(I read a lot of cynical philosophers back then.)

Decades later (many of them), I annually search
For school shoes, shoes that will teach me how
To live inside the skin I seem to have grown into.

Like the galumpy Great Dane puppies, foot size
Is no longer relevant to the rest of me. Either
The shoe fits, or I fit, and, either way, I have to
Be somehow grateful I can walk uphill, downhill,
Cross the Tarmac to a waiting plane, climb stairs,
Navigate a gangway to a small coastal steamer,
Even dance a stately waltz now and then, if asked.

Please, ask me?

My Daughter Throws a Party

Nothing important happened before you were born.

It's Saturday night. The kitchen windows gleam
With wetness from the cookpots' rising steam
And vermicelli coils,
When plunged as water boils,
Making a pattern of pasta basketry
To hold the fragrant treasure of your saucery,
Scenting the air with many little herbs
And buds and spices; nothing here that curbs
The seeking bounds of sweet imagination
Or simplicity of starved appreciation.

Your guests are hungry, may not even know
You washed and ironed this cloth, spread it just so
To honor them, and still, expecting toasts
From the ruby wine to mar the cloth with festive ghosts
Of this meal once by every crumb consumed,
And every memory shared in your brief history exhumed,
This charmed circle of your chosen friends well met.
Rain beats staccato on the windowpanes, and yet
Nothing can enter here if not invited.
History begins with you – your past unblighted
As your smooth and pearly foreheads are –
You are twelve hundred miles from home, yet not so far!

To My Daughter, On Her 21st Birthday

Of course, you were not meant to stay with us:
We raised you in the house, not unlike seedlings,
And knew the time would come to transplant you,
And worry then about a killing frost,
Or worthless weeds that might get in your way:
Some, falsely pretty, like bindweed that chokes
While blooming with its own fair flowering;
Others, more recognizable as threats,
With jagged, knife-edged leaves, like dandelions.
The time has come: it's June, and seedlings grow.
The roots are strong, and hardier, the plant
Which reaches to the sun, and spreads its leaves.

My Daughter's Room Revisited

Coward, I had avoided it,
Ever since you left:
Your room, your place inviolate,
Stripped as if
There'd been a swift theft.

Now, weaponed with feather duster,
Purpose personified,
And all the courage I can muster
I cross the threshold,
Eyes shocked wide.

What you chose to leave behind!
What you did not take!
Secret, small treasures
Everywhere remind of
What you *could* forsake.

Have these no claim on your now
And future role?
Silent and serene, making a small bow,
The Japanese costume doll,
Patient as a wife
Expecting a rambling mate's return,
Untouched by change,
Not yet aware you will not come back
Again in your same girlish guise;
But the animals, your old allies
Against bad dreams, still yearn—
Their whimsical furry pose
Does not admit estrangement.
And the chessboard made of onyx
Brought back from Mexico—
Should that not be part of your new mix,
And go where you will go?

You are a woman, worthy grown,
And must decide yourself what's trash,
What's treasure;
        I only wish I knew how you will measure.

My Grandmother's Hymnal

So green are its covers, like oxidized bronze,
The gilt lettering worn thin,
But Grandmother's hymnal is precious to me
For sweet memories therein.

"The Church in the Wildwood" still echoes today,
"Abide with Me" buttresses trust;
And "Work for the Night Is Coming" leads me
To greet each new day, as I must.

My Grandmother left this temporal world
Full many a year ago;
Her spirit sustains me, and this, her dear book,
Whose hymns _I_ now love and know.

Lullaby

Sleep. For while I love you
Nothing of the earth shall harm you,
Nothing of the day or of the night.

In the glare of the sun, my hand
Will shield your eyes until it burns,
And then it will not fall. Sleep.

In the lash of the storm, my back
Will cut the cold until it freeze,
And then it will not bend. Sleep.

Sleep. But while I love you,
Nothing of the earth shall have you;
Nothing else will ever set you free.

Leo Learns to Read

First of all, you have to understand
He looks like a Raphael cherub:
The inevitable halo forms when sun
Glints off his golden curls.
All this, of course, is misleading!
Leo in real life is a 3-year-old boy,
As full of mischief as any other.
He "reads" to his grandmother,
Having memorized his favorite books.
He knows what grandmothers like:
So Leo turns all the monsters
Into mischievous 3-year-old boys!

Once Upon Another Time 1

Once upon another time,
Unrelenting anger makes
My reluctant memory
Prod proud conscience,
And do retakes
Of just such a day as this:
Setting sun, dark clouds, and we,
Each of us ahurt in her own way,
Neither feeling she
Can risk opening boxed emotions,
And releasing a peace-dove,
Going off to sleep still bruised,
Yet unrelentingly.
One word sighed, inaudibly, by both,
Spontaneously.
"Love," we breathed, and built
A fragile bridge
To lead us back.
Swaying in that storm,
The bridge held – and yet,
It always, after, showed a crack.

Once Upon Another Time 2

To my Mother with Love.

Passing that gate which might have led us out of this,
We are uncertain
In our confrontation.
Frozen, we are, and wishing both to hurt and not;
Taking a shaky breath,
You begin, and bequeath
Me: courage. What you tell me is not startling news:
I am agreeable, you say,
Only when events go my way.
Let me be crossed, and I may show a character
Woefully deficient
In all save impudence. Your aim is true; this clear-cut case of
overkill,
Having been shot before,
Expires upon the floor.
That gate we passed is locked again. Laughter's the key.

Once Upon Three Times

To my daughter.

What would have happened, had I not said, "No"?
Would we have shared a feeling smooth as silk,
With decorous ripples in a curtained fall,
Concealing everything not quite polite?
Instead, this scratchy, shabby, low-grade rage,
So thick a texture, it becomes a pall—-
So suffocating that it makes me gasp.
I cannot bear it willingly, nor still
The sickness in my heart. Unfair, <u>unfair.</u>
To match me, most reluctant combatant,
With you, fierce challenger of all my views?
A child should take in with her mother's milk
The mystery that, did I <u>not</u> love
<u>I would not have, so often, to say, "No."</u>

Birthday Blessing

We change, the wily scientists avow,
Once every seven years—
So you begin another life from now:
Adventure reappears
On far horizons never viewed before.
How do you read the sky,
As wayfarer and traveler once more?
What, with your artist's eye,
Do you perceive, interpret, then evaluate?
You rush toward destiny!
We wish you only a rewarding fate:
A Mozart symphony;
A Summer sky without a darkening cloud;
A picnic in the park;
A friend to share what you dare say aloud;
A candle for the dark.

Old Echoes

Around the festive board, old faces missed
Replace themselves with new ones: likeness-kissed—
The sweetness of a certain curve of cheek;
The tone of voice when one is heard to speak;
The grave regard of granite-colored eyes
Repeat the portraits on the wall; surprise
The senses with a spurt of memory
That answers every questing enquiry
(As potent as the scent of a pressed rose!).
How does a child reflect an aunt's repose
Who never saw her mentor, long at rest,
But read her yellowed diary, frightened lest
The pages crumble in her smooth, young hand?
A boy who knew not his ancestral land
Still bears the stamp of mountains and fjords;
The music's in his bones—the primal chords.
All that we have become, we owe the old
Who went before—their warmth would pierce the cold
Of this year's end and grey December day,
Where past has more than present words to say.

Washday

Long years ago, so many
They are tinged with rose and gilt,
And distorted as if viewed
Through a telescope's other end,
I loved Mondays, most of all
When the sun's bright warmth
And the wind's secret whispers
Made magic of Washday.
For it was then that my mother
Would ask me to help
By handing her clothespins
As she shook out and spread
Every single wrinkled wad to dry:
The sheets billowed like sails
And towels became signal flags—
What message did they send?

I know I was still quite small
(needing to reach up for her hand)
But the message did not escape me.
Some sheets were patched; some
Towels were worn to cleaning rags,
But, flapping in a favorable gust,
All bore brave testimony:
We may gather smudge and stain
Every other day, but on Washday
We are clean again, our colors
Jaunty, and ready to take on
One more week's assault
By soot and smoke and random
Happenings not even mothers could prevent.

Summer Song

For Patricia Davis 1959-1985

When all the world's washed new again,
After the storm,
When breezes drenched with scent of rain
Senses inform,
Then, that small brook beneath the bridge
Rolls toward its spill,
And fills the lake, its primal pledge
Sworn to fulfill.
The water wheel upon the verge
Turns and returns:
What falls will rise; what floats, submerge--
Watching, one learns
That green, the color of our youth,
Color of hope, slips far beyond our mortal truth,
Out of our scope.
But see the sunset sails afloat –
Yes, mark them well!
The Summer caught in one frail boat,
Riding the swell!

On such does memory depend
To turn Time's enemy to friend.

Early Snow, Country Churchyard

How like pillows the headstones seem,
Edges softened by a feathery Fall snow;
Names chiseled in New England granite
Are secrets waiting to be found again
Since we, after all, did return to them.
It's up to us to brush away the early snow,
Leave a little tribute of a rose for each,
Its red a bright stain against the white--
As if to evidence obscure blood ties.

Our frugal forefathers were simple folk,
So we assume of them their stones were
Simple, too—but we are very wrong.
Across our path falls the sudden shadow
Of a tree trunk carved out of grey granite,
Each branch another name, magnificent
Monstrosity-- but plainly here forever!

We fancy we can hear nearby murmurs
(but there are no people here, only beds
for eternity): "Wicked extravagance!"
Someone mutters, and "Ayuh, that it is!"
New Englanders all, their disapproval
Set in stone, as they say, minds set, too.

Every plot has little stones for babies,
Some with angels to guide them home;
Many never grew to play in fresh snow
Or roll in new-cut grass in Summertime.

For those whose dates show they were shriven
On such a day as this, let them be forgiven.
What does it matter now, what did it ever?
When human follies and their ties must sever?

Close to My Heart

Revealing a streak of hidden sentimentality…

Abundance

This day seems too full to lift:
Its possibilities may spill over.
There is an errant breeze to toss
The greening boughs of the oldest trees;
Their folded leaves like origami boxes
Hiding eternal secrets of seasons' changes.

Between what wants to reawaken, be reborn,
And what may want to slumber on awhile
Exists a tension I cannot ease or resolve,
But, with this new, blank, hopeful calendar
I try again to take the day, and make it mine.

Four O'clock Tea

Graceful, the amber arc of tea
Poured from the silver spout
Makes a confluent symmetry:
Warm within, chill without.

You are a special person born
Honored, once you are here.
Archaic as the unicorn,
Ceremony's veneer.

Tea is a fortress of a rite,
Stronger than a sturdy stone;
Made for the jaded soul's delight,
From cottage up to throne.

Waiting

A poem is waiting
At the other end,
The only open end,
Of a maze unbroken
Yet by this or any
Other poet, pleasing
In its placid symmetry
But needing assault,
A change in strategy
To reach the ultimate
Prize: what waits there
Expressed at its best.
This is not it, not yet,
But rhythms coiled
And sinuous, like
Striations of the brain,
Wound tight, ready
To spring, are forming.
Wind has blown downed
Cottonwood and maple
Leaves, like hearts and
Hands, over the privet
Hedge, pointing the way.

Evensong

Let the little songs that beat all day like whirring wings
against the air—
Their gentleness no protest to the shrieking noise,
Montage of traffic, factory whistles, all discordant, strident
blare—
Let the muted sweetness of them now be given a belated
voice.
And let all ears accustomed to the point of self-inflicted deaf-
ness to
Anything that shrieks, let them (oh, most of all!) be reached
by something new.

Bivouac

My dearest dust! Ten years since you have left,
And still when I slip from the bonds of day
To sleep, to dream, I do not feel bereft.
You were not made of such a common clay
That I could let you, precious dust, be blown
By random winds from North to South and back.
Your face is still the young one I have known,
Safe in my heart's embattled bivouac.
A shuttered locket image tells it true—
Though gently can I bear to face it now:
You took off life like some old coat that you
No longer needed, pain smoothed from your brow.

In this place, where my heart resides, I stay
And from my love of yesterday not sway.

Biography

The purity of line
Is woven in the blankets;
Colors of earth,
Colors of sky.
The spirit there,
In warp and weft,
And used therefore
For living,
For dying,
And all the needs between.
The blankets used
To make a shelter
From strong sun,
To wrap a baby,
To warm an Old One,
To make a bed
Beneath the stars...
And, finally,
A winding-sheet
That the Great Spirit
Recognizes
This was one who trod
His ways...and did it well.

Broken Things

There must be a reason, a coolly considered reason,
For keeping a broken object that can be repaired,
Against all odds. The Wedgwood cup cannot be
Returned to its former usefulness, its handle off,
But it can be made to look pretty again, and hold
A small plant like a possibility, a small hope.

Promises, though, even half-promises
Are different. How to repair a promise broken
In the heat of anger or disappointment? And if,
Even if, a misplaced sense of trust could believe
In the remorse of its breaker, how to get back
To the Eden that existed before the promise broke?

Breakers on the shore, relentless as they may seem,
Can sometimes be broken waves if tides have
Changed, or undertow shifted the contours of sand.
Rocks would be good, where breakers come ashore,
But breakers cannot, of course, break rock—
It's quite the opposite effect, in fact.

Breaking bread together means unity,
But breaking up means being apart,
Never, perhaps, to see each other again.
How is it, do you suppose, that I end up
At this stage of life with a box overfull
Of objects that need, that yearn to be
The way they once were, to be fixed
By a sure hand and to be regarded
With an optimistic smile?
                              All is not lost.

Starting Lineup of My Saints

On such a day as this, I line you up
And ask for your protection because
I can no longer make it by myself,
And can't imagine how I ever thought
I could. Agatha and Alexius, kind
Nurses both, pray deliver me
From the disease of greed. Anthony,
Patron saint of lost objects, please
Help me find what I have lost:
I know not how much or where,
But my soul seems to be shrunken.
Cecilia, deliver me from cacophony
And let me hear your music yet again—
I heard it once but seem to have mislaid
This blessing along with many others,
My mercenary focus leading me astray.
Dorothea, from life devoid of flowers,
Deliver me and let me play in your
Fields with joy I once long ago knew.
Eligius, patron saint of goldsmiths,
I ask not for your gold but heaven's,
The rays that show themselves after
A storm is over. From avaricious
Eyes, deliver me once again.
Fiacre, you love your taxi-drivers;
Please love me, too, a passenger
Along life's convoluted route.
Isidore of Seville, you of cyberspace,
From crashes and such, deliver me,
And leave me a little wiser each time
My miraculous machine runs amok.
For all your care, I thank you, saints,
And please tell your sisters, the angels
Whom I love, too, I need all of you.

The Cracks in the Glaze

This pitcher, made from earth, yet mirrors sky:
That crystalline, pure blue of wind-washed air.
Its surface bears a maze of tiny cracks,
A labyrinth of lines etched in the glaze.

It is a little history of life—
For here it was set down too hard, and there
It suffered from a surfeit of such use
One wonders how it could be filled again
And pour as freely as it did before
The limitless libations it has known:
To celebrate,
To slake the thirst,
To ease
More somber celebrations to their ends...

At last, to sit upon the middle shelf
Regarded reverentially for worth
It did not have
When it was shining new.

Blest with Myopia

Morning. Myopic mist, visible light...
Without my glasses, all is beautiful.
It's true that everything has soft edges,
And shapes assume new forms even
As they're recognized: hatracks turn
Into the tallest and thinnest of people.
Well, good, I think: guest for breakfast,
How pleasant! And he/she doesn't look
To be a greedy eater, lucky for a hostess
Who doesn't stock great larders
Full of food.

Without glasses, I can admire
A sunlit shaft and notice not dustmotes
That surely must be floating there, where
The most casual housekeeper would whisk
Away such evidence of sloth. Blissfully
Unaware, I simply prize the sparkle coaxed
From old lead crystal when the sunlight hits.
Mornings have been this way for me forever,
And every day I thank a Kind Providence
For gifting me with this apparent flaw
Which makes my world so luminous it takes
My breath away. . . until I pick up the paper
And feel around for my despised spectacles,
To see more clearly the other side of the news.

Wind Chimes

Out of the air is born
This sonorous soliloquy
On such a sleepy Summer day!
Into the velvet void of night
Are tossed random notes
To play among the stars.

The Tapestry

The houses on our street are haunted by
The ghosts of little children who grew up
And moved away—the houses seem to sigh
For them. Our sidewalks bear no faintest hop-
Scotch chalking. Rusted swing sets, empty, move
In Summer's slightest breeze. A garden shows
A crooked flower bed, designed by love
And hands too small to dig straight. All that grows
Must change. But one thing stays the memory—
Firm woven, of tight threads: a tapestry.

String of Pearls

For the Glenn Miller fans at Nutley High, Class of 1943

We were all graduated pearls, I think,
Some just more lustrous than the rest of us,
But strung into a single strand of thread,
Unbroken by the hopes and dreams we shared.

That time we knew will never come again,
However hard we chase our vanished youth,
Yet there are traces in those gathered here:
Fine faces, with their history inscribed.

For we were still unfinished at eighteen,
The sheen of polishing by passing years
Was missing then. Now look around: admire
The silver setting of the pearls we were!

Passing the Time

At 912 Sixteenth Street,
A round, imposing clock
That reminds of long-ago
Mayors and councilmen,
Those with a wide expanse
Of vest over full stomachs,
A pocket watch of gold
And its heavy links of chain.

This doughty clock has stood
For a hundred years and more,
Carefully wound each day
By a trusted workman with a key
So enormous it might open doors
Of sacred cities, but here it winds
Only the Kortz Jewelers clock,
The purpose for which it was made.

Heading North I pass regretfully,
Wishing I could stay and admire
The Kortz clock's elegant lines,
Its delicate hands keeping count
Of every second of every minute
Of every day. In an uncertain world,
This sentry of Sixteenth Street
Stays calm amid winds of change
As if they never even happened.

Breaking News

Pristine as it seems pre-opening,
This crisply folded morning paper hides
Too many secrets, some unsavory.

Breaking news, as they say,
Waits within the folds to be
Found out, to make eyebrows
Fly up like gulls' wings,
To bring a blush upon the cheek.

What else awaits discovery?
Headlines for sports employ
Action verbs, to say the least:
Semi-brutes of words they are,
Evoking images of hard-hitting
Blows from bludgeons or from fists.

There are softer stories, no less urgent,
Of life and death waged on a desert plain:
A mother soothes her starving child,
Rocks and sings, for no milk is left
And comfort is all she has to offer.

So, is this breaking news, do you think?
It happens every hour of every day,
As constant as the tides of the sea.

Heart-breaking news.

Cats Wander In and Out and In Again

Just how they are. Never quite content with the way of the world...

Cat as Simile and Metaphor

Like a small, grey cat,
Ephemeral as a puff of smoke,
This poem sidled up to me,
Rubbing against silken ankles
In a sweet, insistent way—
Here to stay, like it or not.

There were other claims on me:
My time, a "To Do" list waiting.
But never mind all that on this day
Of the cat. Who knows when the wind
May blow a puff of smoke my way again?

It did not happen yesterday,
And may not recur tomorrow;
So come here, cat; let me make
A lap for you. Stay with me awhile.

White Cat in a Snowsquall

I know a cat is in there somewhere!
I look out upon the winter backyard,
Picnic table empty but for a tall cake,
An angel food, perhaps, but snow;
Swing set holding a passenger load of
Snowpeople; slide all too slippery
With its layers of ice and snow, snow
And ice. The cat has left her signature
Prints following bird claw tracks
On the nearly virgin snow. At one point,
Bird tracks disappear and that's probably
A trophy feather darkening
The area around it. Cat can't be far;
She's probably hiding under shelter
Of the woodpile, savoring her catch.

Library Lion

Regal, noble the lions who guard
The New York City Library
At 42nd & 5th, figure in my visions
Of that city which I visit more often
In dreams than in reality. They have
Names: Patience and Fortitude,
Bestowed on them by a Depression-era
Mayor to hearten his unemployed
Millions. That's New York.

This is Denver. In the Southeast corner
Of this city is a much smaller guardian
For the branch library. He is unimposing:
Grey tabby, curled into a question mark
On the sun-warmed wall behind a bench
Where the most eager readers await
The daily opening of the doors.

His name is whatever the children call
Him. He answers to "Yo!" as well as
The ubiquitous "Kitty" from the smallest
Kids, who don't liken WINNIE THE POOH
To pets hearthside. He likes to listen to
The six-year-old reviews: "Tigger's not a
Real cat, not like one you'd meet on
Your block." "Yeah, but the whole book
Is pretend. Like WIND IN THE WILLOWS.
No cats there, either. Not regular ones."

A teenage boy's voice, heard
On the brink of breaking, says,
"Just wait a while. When you're
A bit older, you can read T. S.
Eliot, Rudyard Kipling, Dr. Seuss,
May Sarton. These dudes all had
Cats in their books. You'll see."

The little library lion goes on duty.
He stretches his miniature muscles,
Prepared to defend his castle of books
Against any cynical comers who ever
Doubt that love and cats conquer all.

Moths as Cat Toys

Beneath the porch light
A dozen or so moths
Are so pleased with
Themselves they can
Taunt the alert cat
Who wants to catch
And taste one of the
Moth air force. Just
For fun. He has no
Grudge against the
Moth population.

Cat, we've been through
This before. You reach
And stretch but still
Cannot capture the tiny
Winged creatures. Claws
Get caught in the screen
Door, but, as soon as
You are freed, you go
Back to this fruitless
Pursuit. I despair of
You, I have to say.

Suppose you caught
A moth—surely, this
Has happened—did
You notice how dry,
Like gunpowder, the
Taste taunted your
Tongue? Did you
Wonder where it
Went when you tired
Of your unwinnable
Game? Maybe not.
The moth is drawn
To the light as you
Are to the moths.

Reading My Cat

If my cat were a book, sleek white
Cover with pristine pages enclosed,
I could read her moods more easily.

I know that, when she's embarrassed,
She washes her ears most diligently,
Something I find amusing to watch.
(But I have to stifle my laughter—
Cats detest being made fun of.)

I know that, when she's hungry,
She does this little dance thing
With her paws on the glass part
Of the sliding door; it's adorable.

She has green-gold eyes, mere slits
When she wants to look wise—
Not hard for her to do when she
Tucks paws under chin, resembling
An ancient Chinese Mandarin.

She lives in our hearts as well as
Our home, and it's hard to pretend
We don't miss her when she's elsewhere

A few days at a time. On her return,
She looks like a Mardi Gras reveler—
Raggedy, with a slight hungover head—
And could do with bath, food, and nap.

How pretty she is, how sweetly she
Sleeps! Wonder how many rebounds
She has left to surprise us with?

A Riddle Wrapped in a Mystery

Cats are round and fat of cheek,
Or, cats are long and stretched-out sleek.
Cats have eyes that look oblique
And never straight at what they seek,
But cats are *never* meek.

Cats are never meek because
All cats *know* they have no flaws,
And they have very clever paws
With sheathed or unsheathed, sharpened claws
And do things that demand applause.

Cats demand applause by all
For the way they leap, the way they crawl.
You may have, hiding in your hall,
A tiny tiger from Bengal,
Waiting to pounce at your footfall.

Cats wait to pounce because they must
Practice constantly; they just
Must not miss that perfect mouse; adjust
Perhaps to Meow Mix, trust
You to fill the cat-dish, yet show disgust.

Sometimes, cats show disgust; interpret
This as counterfeit...
If you loved me, they submit,
You'd grant my wish list, every bit—
Until then, they will simply sit.

Cats will simply sit and stare
Waiting for you to be aware
Of needs which they cannot declare.
Do they need a pat or scratch where
They cannot reach? Surely you have a pat to spare
For a cat.

Cats go where they *want* to go,
Wander in shadows, to and fro,
And, in the dark, their eyes will glow.
Cats run fast, and cats creep s-l-o-w;
They know something *we'll* never know.

Cat at the Laundromat

Nobody knows whose cat she is—
But she knows: she is her own cat.
She comes to this steamy place
To find such joy as there may be
Atop a vibrating machine on
Spin-dry cycle that sounds so
Like a mechanical purr.
It's warm, besides, and people
Passing by often give her a pat.
One sentimental soul brings
Dry packets of cat food which
She politely pretends to like.
Who knows? The quality may
Not be the best, but love is ever
The inspiration. *Thank you,*
She purrs. It's cold in the outside
World, but not in here. Nobody
Closes the door against her.
She is the Laundromat cat.

Chess Cat

This is the best of all
Possible places to be
On any Saturday night:
Chess club meets at the
Crossroads Mall. It's
The cat's night out!

He has a certain dignity
About him, a handsome
Tabby coat and golden
Eyes -- yet he is not there
To be seen, but to see.

In this place, the players
All humans) are the most
Like cats as it's possible
For them to be. Watch how
Quiet they are, yet ready to
Spring at their opponents'
Mistakes, to pounce on the
Clock. An entire evening
Can pass like this, from their
Civil greetings to each other,
Through the subdued silent
War on the chessboard, to
The inevitable conclusion
In which one has to win, the
Other must bear the loss,
But always with stoic smiles.

This may be the only uncatly
Aspect of the match. No cat
Smiles unless he means it.

Re-Treed

As if written by Joyce Kilmer's cat.

I think that I shall never see
A tree unclimbable by me.

I sink my claws into the bark,
Perhaps pursuing tuneful lark,
Her song to me not half as sweet
As savoring her matchless meat.

But larks are swift-winged and elude
A cat with this crass attitude.
And now that I have missed my prey,
The ground seems much too far away!

Why do I do it? Why, oh why?
This tree seems to embrace the sky
So tall is it that, if I leap,
My fate will be eternal sleep.

Humiliated, stuck, I stay;
Lark lives to sing another day!

A Certain Slant of Light

After the Seattle quake of 2001.

Shattered into shards like mosaic,
The aftermath of earthquake glows
In a glass puddle on the concrete floor,
As if a cat's paw, only playing, swiped
This sunlit wonder from off a tabletop.
Six-point-eight on the Richter scale
Or eight-pounds-six of cat, same fate.

Before the quake, these glass anemones
Bloomed into bowls and shapes not made
To serve any appetite excepting only this:
The hungry soul. Some were like flowers,
Yes, and some seashells with scalloped rim,
And fancies beyond the functional familiar.
All orchestrated tones of light within, without.

Call it not destruction, rather rebirth. Just how
A certain slant of light strikes is a new wonder.

The Cat's Mouse

An Allegory.

Shiny and sleek as ripe eggplant,
But bigger, much bigger, is My Cat.
Yet she walks with feather step
So none may hear her coming, none
Excepting only me. My outsize ears,
Like satellite dishes, pick up everything
I need to know to stay alive. Twitching
Whiskers signal danger, not from My Cat,
At whose pleasure I survive, of course.

Being the pet of a pet is not easy. Someday
My Cat may forget what fun I provide
And I will meet that fate of all fates,
Not greatly to be desired. We have rules,
My Cat and I. If I follow with respect
My little span may stretch beyond today.

Which is all that a 3-inch, 2-ounce mouse
Can reasonably wish for: a chance to try
The delights of crumbs from party trays
Not yet pounced upon by Management,
At whose pleasure I survive, remember.

Upper Management would not give me
One more day upon this planet, yet does
Not My Cat, only Middle Management
To the humans who share our house,
Protect me, while giving the illusion
Of The Hunt and Kill Game? I live because
My Cat lets me. Without her, I would
Be lured into a trap by a chunk of Cheddar,
And pass unnoticed and unremarked
Into a lesser Limbo. The smaller humans
In our house are programmed to like mice,
As witness the mega-mouse named Mickey.

But this affection does not go beyond
Childhood, and children are not even
Considered Middle Management; they have
No vote to say who shall live, who shall die.

My Cat is thus my hero as well as my cause for
Anxiety. I know my place. If I must amuse, I amuse.
I do my job as if my life depends on it. It really *does*.

Church Cats

On almost any Sunday
You can track my walk
To church by the cats
Who come out to greet
Me. The silver bells ring
Out and the signal is heard.
This slows my pace, never
Swift, to a mere stroll,
Because the cats need pats
And compliments. Who can
Deny them such small favors?

From the big orange tabby
To the sleek little Siamese,
These church cats have their
Own places, like familiar
Pews, from where come mews
Of differing pitches: the most
Strident from the small Siamese—
Who would imagine that much
Sound could come from such a
Tiny body! The tabby is fat and
Mellow with a disproportionate
Delicate voice, just right for "Amen."

Crying in the Rain

The small, demure grey cat next door
I imagine to be Emily Dickinson's ghost.
She is so tidy, cuffed in white paws,
It saddens me to see her caught in the rain,
Her fur in tufts, crying to get in.

"I know, I know, Emily!" I tell her softly,
Soft as a purr. "But they love you.
The door will open." She quiets and tilts
Her decorous little head a few degrees,
Seemingly intent on understanding.

The rain has caught me unawares, as well,
And once I would have tried to drink it in,
But, now, it makes my angular bones ache.
And there is no use crying at the door,
For no one's on the other side to let me in.

Notice now: raindrops and tears are often
So alike they fuse. Who can say where
One leaves off and the other begins?

Perennial Catalogue

Cat of my heart, fine furry friend,
Somehow I fail to comprehend:
Why is the sofa torn and clawed
But your old scratching-post unpawed?

And can you tell me, dearest puss
(More puzzling than an abacus)
Why tuna fish is fine, Friday –
But, Saturday, no more, no way!

Thank you for bringing from outdoors
Many nice mice (all dead, of course);
Pray do not notice I turn green
Despite the numbers I have seen.

Little fur person whom I love,
Most precious treasure of my trove,
Would your bad habits be sore-missed
Could we but, peaceful, co-exist?

Paw Prints on the Porsche

This is a superb machine, this car,
Occupying two parking spaces
To avoid even the least of scratches
On its dazzling fourteen coats of paint.
The color is named for a famous opera;
Who could wish for a better passport
To the high life? There is a minor flaw:
La Boheme portrays the life of artists
Traditionally impoverished, so a KIA
Might be a better symbolic choice
Than a Porsche. At least, consider it.

There is, however, one equalizer noted
With the muddy paw prints of a small cat
Distributed impartially across the hood.
The cat's inbred elegance and curiosity
Magnetized it to decorating your car.
The motor must have been still warm,
So the cat curled up for a nap right there,
The graffiti of little cat feet is left behind.

Where is this culprit? You look all around
The scene of the crime, at last discovering
A tidy marmalade cat of fastidious nature
Carefully licking mud off her pretty paws,
Her mysterious eyes wise slits revealing
Not a trace of remorse, far less apology.
Cats are formed without a moral compass.

Cats just *are*.

Haiku for Cats

Hidden Source of sound
In tall grass: cat's ears prick up,
Eyes become searchlights.

Wind-tossed rosebush calls
To cat to play; she lunges
To catch a branch: Ouch!

Before kite is launched,
Cat must test its tail of rags,
Leaps after take-off.

Cat loves holidays:
Bags and boxes to hide in,
Rainbows of ribbons.

Sewing lesson starts:
Silver needle flashes bright:
Cat makes leaps of joy!

Fat robin warbles,
Cat enjoys concert – but then
Cannot resist fate!

Their revels over
Two cats must form Yin and Yang
On sunbaked flagstone.

Creature Comforts

Of all the animals—and those who hunt them…

McCauley's Bear

After a painting by Robert McCauley, "Out There on The Clearcut II."

"What did you have to do <u>that</u> for?"
This bemused bear seems to ask,
And with good reason. A golden
Swarm of honeybees had brought
Him a rare gift: a honeycomb he
Had immediate plans for, on sight.

To bite into the abundant wax and
Chew, savoring every bit of honey,
For starters. He might even have
Prudently put half of it away for
Next time hunger strikes. He might.

We will never know now, will we?
You carelessly brushed a honeybee
Away from your face, and he stung
In retaliation, taking the swarm away
With him for the little span of living
He has yet to know. You were hurt,
You admitted, and so thoughtless.
But he, the hero bee, is now dying.

And McCauley's bear stands in the
Clearing, trying to remember how
Honey licked straight from the comb
Tastes so much better than other honey.
The bear is still hungry, you sense,
Edging away step by backwards step,
As if in the presence of royalty,
Telling yourself black bears are not
Carnivores, and attack only when angry.

Which he might be: only one way
To find out. Clearly, since you were
The one to swat at the bee, you ought
To be the designated bear-baiter. It did
Start out to be a beautiful, sunny day.
That may not last much longer.

Beach Poem With Dogs

Consider the sand with your first step:
How it catches the print of your foot,
Even to its high-arched architecture,
Done by a Master of functional design.

Sand may seem almost too white,
Too fine-grained—but remember
That this is how concrete evolves.
What seems abstract here and now
Extrudes itself into new shapes, coiled
And convoluted, like a nautilus shell.

Down at water's edge, sheer lace
Like Battenburg rims the white foam.
See how nothing can last, here:
Your footprints washed away, yes,
Your markings alongside sandpipers'
And gulls' and paw prints from dogs
Chasing waves, barking at them
Futilely, but still, always on duty.
Dogs!

Plant your beach umbrella as if
It were a rare, gigantic bloom—or,
Better yet, a flag to mark a 14er.*
Spread out an old, worn blanket,
Useful for lying on while drying off.

That's if the dogs shaking selves
Dry don't shower you like spray
From the ocean yet again.
Dogs just want you to hunker
Down awhile, be more like them.
You give up nothing, not power
Or prestige, to toss a Frisbee.

(*a mountain higher than 14,000 ft.)

The Predator and the Prey

Springtime, the Return of the Flicker.

He *is* the predator, my house his prey.
Probably no bigger than the average cat,
His wingspread still impressive,
Songless, this bumbling bird beats
Staccato, like some crazed drummer
Or a hard-hat with pneumatic drill.

He seems to stomp upon my roof
And eaves; he cannot glide, but lands
With thump as though he lost velocity
Along with anything resembling song.
His drumming says, "Come, my love,
I have a perfect place for us to share!"

My house has holes in it now, randomly
Assayed for nesting spots or edible bugs,
Reasons no real-estate agent would believe.
My house has weathered winds and storms,
Many years of living and loving, but this?
This I take as assault on my venerable
House that I have vowed to keep safe, insure,
Paint, glaze, keep from predator's harm.

What I can do, I have done: Ridiculous,
My means of combat streamers of foil,
Spiraled ribbons of spectacular hues,
Whistles I have blown; echoes of drills
I have rapped on the window to scare
The creature off; he stays, he drums on.

But suddenly the cat, roused from a nap
By the bird's sound and my fury, stalks
As if my backyard were a jungle, eyes
Mere slits, hissing with dramatic flair.
Bird chooses: —carpentry or cat? —and is gone.

All the Pretty Little Horses

"Hush-a-bye, and don't you cry,
Go to sleepy, little baby—
When you awake, you shall have cake,
And all the pretty little horses. . ."

From an Appalachian lullaby

They feel it first, the colts and ponies do,
The very essence of a Rocky Mountain spring.
You see them shake their manes and sniff the air,
Their shaggy coats become more glossy now;
Perked ears take on alertness for a certain sound,
And, questioning, their eyes grow much too bright,
As, prancing their delight, they trot the pasture round.
Just at the meadow's edge, an old fruit tree
Still blossoms. Wind makes petals into pink snowfall,
This season which is both an end and start,
And oh! The pretty little horses love it all.

Done with Mirrors

As the magician's pretty assistant
Used to say, smiling provocatively,
"It's all done with mirrors."

I think of that when I view
My face in the bathroom mirror,
Especially after a shower which
Leaves everything wreathed in
A fine mist. It's my favorite mirror
Because it's soft focus.

The bedroom mirror overhead,
On the other hand, is merciless.
Shadows do not obscure but
Seem to sharpen the cheekbones
And brow, and lines radiate
Recklessly from eyes to mouth
And back again. It's impossible
To believe six impossible things
About oneself before breakfast,
In the bedroom mirror.

The kitchen has a fun mirror. It
Doesn't mean to be taken seriously,
But it says, on its corner,
"You look *mahvelous!*" It's a leftover
From gym class in high school,
When there was never enough time.
There is still not enough time,
But to see the reassuring message
On the way to answering the doorbell
Is not nothing.

I think the time may have come,
Sneaking into my consciousness
While I lay defenseless, asleep,
To say, "**I'm** done with mirrors."

Night Lights

The hour is three: that harrowing time
Post-midnight, pre-dawn, narrowing
Down to the least possibility of sleep.

Warm milk with honey equals rescue:
You pad out to the kitchen—but stop!
Ombered shadows are punctuated by
The smallest of lights, unnoticed by day:
Green monitors the sleeping computer,
The VCR, the cable TV, the air purifiers,
Insect repellers, even the passive phone,
Not ringing now, but ready for anything.
Digital clocks' LCDs blush red for shame.
Every high-tech guardian of the house
May, in fact, need human intervention
To get it back on track, after the storms.

You smile at the absurdity of ascribing
Magical powers to your electric servants,
Whose fate depends on you and you alone.
Who is servant here; who is master?

Tiffany Silver Fork From 1895 Meets Frozen Marie Callender

Dear lady, you look so cold! Please warm
Yourself in the microwave, they tell me
This wonderful invention is called. I'm sure
You'll look more like the photo on your box
Once heated up. The text beside the picture
Says, "Complete Chicken Dinner with Two
Vegetables, Including Whipped Potatoes."
How did they get all that into a flat package?

I harken back to the days of five-course meals,
You will remember: appetizer, soup, salad, main
Course and dessert. Now *that* was food I could
Get my tines into! Nor did I have to do it all by
Myself: there was a seafood fork, salad fork, even
A dessert fork. You see my delicate shell pattern?
It was the very dickens to polish, but there was
No lack of willing hands to take care of the silver.

I seem to recall busy hands actually preparing
The food, scrubbing, peeling, shredding, mixing—
No possible way such a meal could fit in a box!
I must have been used thousands of times over
And still, you see, my tines, though worn a bit,
Are still strong enough for any challenge. I do
Wonder about this Marie Callender, though. What
If I struck a frozen portion and it bent my tines?

But be of good cheer. It's better to be useful,
Don't you agree, than to lie in a storage tray
With perhaps a polishing cloth for company,
To be taken out only on special occasions?
I am, after all, a minor celebrity: a Tiffany Shell
Pattern fork, marked on my back: Sterling Silver.
I'm lucky to have survived to take my place in
Modern times, even to eat Marie Callender meals!

Bird Calls

The rocks are ribs; the ridges form
The spine, to make a mountain live:
And trees that bend before a storm
Seem breathing entities that thrive
On earth and water, air and fire;
Anatomy is like this land,
The structure is the skeleton
Which one must fully understand
As did the artist, Audubon,
Who brought us news about the birds,
Who feathered their frail bones for flight,
Who favored flocks instead of herds;
Who saw eternity alight
In guise of pure-white winged dove,
The first from Noah's Ark to bring
A message of forgiving love.
Birds are the voices; they can sing
In language always understood.
Birds are the hope, ethereal thrust
Of what we might be, if we could—
Or, what we can be, if we must.
What other creatures show the way,
Inscribed in arcs across the sky?
Let him who thinks he stands, they say,
Be wary lest he fall awry;
Such little sermons on the wing
Are lost on those who cannot sing.

The Creatures: Busybody

The Navajo equivalent of "busybody":
Someone who tells sheep which weed to eat.

Because the world is full of straying sheep,
At least as far as Angus is aware,
The border collie does not dare to sleep.

The valley floor is dense with heather, deep:
When trod upon, it scents the evening air—
Because the world is full of straying sheep.

Like some old vicar, now must Angus keep
His vigil, sensing peril everywhere:
The border collie does not dare to sleep.

Nearby, a wolf may chance to bide, to creep
From out his hidden mountain lair
Because the world is full of straying sheep.

But Angus watches while the lambkins leap
To save his flock from being Lobo's fare,
And keep them from the verdant mountain steep
Because the world is full of straying sheep.

Punctuation Poems

*Struggles with the stubborn offenders of clarity and
"comma" sense...*

Ampersand & All That

Place it on the page, one half-loop
Atop the other, and it's a partial 8.
Or, laid on its side, it becomes more
Like a symbol for infinity. Or, again,
Just let it imply there's more to come.

In my heretic or pagan prayers, I take
Some comfort in such surmise. It may
Indeed mean immortality, or may not
Do more than hint: heaven's possibility.

Whichever eventuates, I will take it as
It comes. Is there time, do you suppose,
For one more poem?

                             &

One more *everything*
Is what my hedonistic heart
Inclines to ask...
As if this planet, green with hope,
Were not enough?

Apostrophe Catastrophe

If you should want to give me fits,
Just put apostrophes in "it's."

You mean possessive, but you stray—
You simply can't say it that way.
For "it's" with that apostrophe
Means only that it *is,* you see.
But "its", pristine and polyglot,
Can tell you who belongs to what.

Asterisky

If you must resort to it, the little star,
Embarrassment like an unwelcome embrace
Takes firm hold of you. You have not
Done your work well if the asterisky
Aspect is self-evident. It means you
Made an omission or commission
It means you need to explain where
And why and perhaps how it went,
This treacherous subterranean layer
In your artfully simple exposition,
Exposition that exposes your flaws.

If you thought you could pull it off,
Think again. The little star signals
Brightly in the desolate dark of night,
The night you wrestled with writing.

Bracketeering

Pairing the most unlikely duos
{for whom there is no other way}
Brackets concern themselves like
Hopeless busybodies with taxes,
With May-December romances,
With historical citings {yawnyawn}
And longwinded literary references.
Who is to say them nay if they bring
Order out of chaos? Except, possibly,
Those who thought chaos more fun,
Who did not welcome any tinkering.

Only the scholars welcome their look,
Sober responsibility on the printed page,
Enriched by arcane Latin abbreviations
Oh, and kindly spare us the translations?

Breaking Up is Hard to Do

If you must, to make things fit,
Hy-phen-a-tion may be *it*.
Re-con-sid-er how you write;
Shorter words may ease your plight.

Commacide

Never place a period where God has placed a comma.
—Gracie Allen

There are so many variants:
The red-white-and-blue comma,
Meant to separate and grant
A breather in the midst of all;
The poet's random commattacks
Reprising e. e. cummings (again)
And commas like hiccups
Surprising even he who commits
Commacide, strewn like rose petals
Along the ceremonial red carpet,
Announcing the arrival of an
Overblown imagery pleasing
Only to political orators or
Fervent preachers, perhaps.
These make the rest of us
Commatose.

A Visit to the Colonies

There are two islands here, of equal
Size: Colon and Semi-Colon. Seen
As if from the air, distantly, they draw
Not only the eye, but the fugitive mind
Which seeks to understand their reason for being.

Yes, there are two of them.
No, they do not duplicate what the other
Is doing. They are like fraternal twins
With differing views, not the same at all.
The colon says: What's coming up is
The nut, the kernel, the very essence
You've been looking and listening for.
"Good," you say, "I can use that." Say on.

The semi-colon loves order as a master
Gardener loves a well-tended lawn, weeds
Of extraneous thought not let in. See how
The semi separates two ideas of equal heft,
Neither more important than the other, both
Needing your simultaneous attentions now.
That aerial metaphor just means
Distance lends enchantment. How else
Could two such similar islands be seen
So sentimentally by you, each with its own
Worth in these small colonies?

The Elusive Ellipses

"Something's missing" is its history;
What that may be remains a mystery.
If language inappropriate's your fear,
The scholar's help, three little dots, is here.
You may well wish to curse a bright blue streak
Without igniting blushes on your cheek:
You merely hint at first letter and last,
And let the reader make his own bombast.
A device most useful in its way,
But what that is...I do not care to say.

Exclamation Explanation!

Look at its sinister shape: stiletto seems
A fair comparison, or maybe scimitar.
Think of one of opera's classic arias
Wherein the baritone falls on his sword
For lack of love from his lady, singing
Full voice and magnificently, too, while
Dying for unrequited love. (The tenor always
Gets the girl in opera.) What this poor fellow
Needs is a new-coined punctuation mark,
Like the dynamically dualed interrobang
What sly, sardonic tones come out of that!
It dares to question the iconic Cagney death
Scene, poor wretch riddled with bullet holes,
Dragging body across screen in final throes.
Our baritone dies, accompanied by full orchestra,
And amazingly hits that final note with bravado
Worthy of "Bravo!" –oh, look, even that has a !

Parenthetical Hypothetical

Say your research netted more of everything
Than you can gracefully use, and say you do
Want to avoid the appearance of pomposity,
Yet still need to be taken seriously by peers.
(Who is my peer? Is not a valid question.)

With these curvy conjectures (this and this)
You may safely toss in any random thoughts
You were too undisciplined to omit before!

Parentheses can add detail inconspicuously.
Is someone Ichabod Cranely in physique?
(Tall, knobby-boned, totally unprepossessing)
Would fill in the verbal portrait for the reader.

Your sympathies for the losing sports heroes
Could be expressed between the rounded lines
(This was the fifth loss for the team this year),
Boosting fans' fading loyalties, squeezing out
A lachrymose liquid from the eye (i.e., a tear).

The Period

Its finality is a fact,
Not negotiable as,
Say, a semi-colon
Might be imagined.

It's fair warning
That the end is
In sight. Detours
Are possible (like
Parentheses), or
The spirited dash--
But once you arrive
At that Fatal period,
It all but announces:
𝕽epent, for the en𝖉
𝕴s here.

The Question Mark

Surely, some of the most significant
Happenings in the world's and your
History have hinged on questions or
The answers to them. Consider:

"Do you love me?"

"Are you asking me to marry you?"

"Does our insurance cover a baby?"

"You served last time. Do you have to go?"

"Sir, have you heard rumors of surrender?"

"Theirs, not ours?"

"Didn't we pray for this day?"

"Did you miss me?" "Why's the baby crying?"

"Is it because she only knows my picture?"

Umlauts öh, nö!

I must admit to having certain doubts
About the usefulness of most umlauts.
"Coördination" makes its case, of course;
It could be worse: the ø sound in Old Norse.
Consider how we pussyfoot around
The diphthong, quite uncertain of its sound.
Yet even that is easier to say—
I'll take its swerving skidmarks any day.

Landscapes, Exterior and Interior

Fine-grain prints of the difference in what is seen, and felt, and allowed to be shown…

The Broadmoor Revisited

A Journey Back in Time.

When Maxfield Parrish painted it,
From red roofs down to porte-cochere,
A dome of blue infinity
Like a glass bell-jar covered all.
The gauzy chiffon ladies lit
The evening air, their voices silvery
As filigree; their satin shoes
Scuffed secrets on the parquet floors.
The orchestra played "Avalon"
And Scott Fitzgerald's golden boys
Brought champagne to their Daisy-girls.

Down marble halls of time today
The ectoplasmic echoes ring,
As from the tennis courts a bounce
Of youth and strength reverberates,
And still the maitre d' who stands
Beside the Garden Room's green door
Bemoans the passing of true style,
As dieters replace gourmets
And nobody knows wine these days.

Ducks on Lollipop Lake

The little lake is rimmed with rime,
Yet in its deepest center, ripples flow.
There, warmth's retained, from endless Summer days;
The ducks remember Summer, so they go—
Aglide, as graceful as swan-sisters now—sail!
As ballerinas waddle when they walk,
When that mysterious message comes to flock
And fly to kinder climates when the turn
Of treacherous seasons comes! They catch the heart
With their well-ordered numbers taking flight.
Of that same universe, we are a part,
For all that we walk awkwardly at times,
In elements against our natural bent,
And flutter helplessly when we are lost,
And wonder if our faith is fraudulent.
When we know cold, we can remember warm;
Envised by pain, release is pleasure pure;
When we are hungry, we are somehow fed,
For all else passes; yet will God endure.

The Garden in March

Now comes the time to test
Our Wintered faith again;
What hope we reinvest
In Spring's harsh regimen!

The earth-encrusted hands;
The knees that kneel, prayerful;
The body's numb demands
To bend and stretch and pull!

But there is, underneath,
The reason for it all—
This tiny plot of heath
Claimed by our tired footfall.

This is our place for such a brevit span!
The dormant bulbs will bloom,
To praise God's faith in man—
His Grace our best heirloom.

Lone Tree at Timberline

They still come back,
The woodchucks and the birds;
They brave fierce winds
To visit me again,
Though there is nothing left
For them to eat.
They chatter and they chirp
As cheerfully
As if a forest feast
Awaited them,
As it did, far below...
And long ago.
The forest may still yield
Some forage there,
But up here, where the earth
Can scarce conceal
My old, tenacious roots,
And I am bent
In labyrinthine lines,
A silhouette
Of question marks that ask:
How long have I?
How long before the wind
Claims all my sap, my life?
The edelweiss,
That little plant of hope,
Goes on...and on.

Mathematica

Written in the shadows of war.

By little pieties of X and Y,
The organist plays Bach
As if it were a liturgy:
Lamb of God, have mercy
Upon us and grant us peace...
There is a celestial labyrinth
Within Bach's counterpoint
More convoluted now than
When it was composed,
Coiled as any Nautilus shell,
Sounds within sounds,
Spiral within spiral.
Where the organist's hands
Contact keyboard and stops
Exists a very potent chemistry,
One to flare up and set afire
Our seeking, immortal souls.
Echoes within the chapel walls:
Have mercy ... grant us peace!

Postcard from Colorado

The sky is like an endless tent of blue –
The distant mountains, rocks to hold it down.
Beneath this tent, the spectator becomes
Participant in what he otherwise
Might just observe. He walks a mountain trail,
And shares his backpack snack with denizens
Of forest and of air...the silence sings!
His tread on fallen needles from the pines
May be the loudest sound he hears all day.
A valley vista spreads itself below
Where he has climbed, a little ridge to reach
And crow about triumphantly, until
A golden eagle soars into his view,
With nothing but the wind to ride upon.
At close of day, he sits in his motel,
Trail-dust all washed away, in clean, new clothes.
He tries to write a message to his friends
On scenic postcards, brighter than real life;
What can he say to them, make them believe?
The postcard measures four inches by five...

Park Picture in Black and White

Like etchings on the sky, the trees stand stark,
No leaves unfurled as banners in the wind
To herald the approach of warmth and Spring.
Still snowfields slow joggers as they run;
Ice islands make small mirrors of the lake.
Yet Winter is not so invincible.
For we see through its fortress opening chinks
Of hope, as when a bravely soaring kite
Takes off, and tugs our hearts aloft with it.
And look: the ducks are back! Too soon, of course,
Those feathered optimists predict a thaw;
Yet who knows but (this time) they may be right?
The creatures without clocks or calendars
May harbor more of wisdom than we know;
And sap wells up within the leaf-lorn trees,
Yes, even while black branches like harpstrings
Stir distant music on a stage of snow.

Trusting the Tide Mark

Kristin Marie is only three, but she's an architect:
Her castle made of sand and popsicle sticks and foil
From ice-cream wrappers and shards of broken glass
Washed smooth by the same sea that invades her beach –
Treasures from trash (grownups don't know everything!)

But should I tell her about the treacherous tide now?
How it will come in overnight and when, next morning,
She looks for her wondrous castle again, it will be gone –
Only a few popsicle sticks and scraps of foil to show
That it was ever there- for all her work and dreams?

No, *not* to tell is best. Kristin would probably say,
"The tide mark shows that's how high God would *let*
The ocean come… and, anyway, I can build another castle."
"And even if I had to do it again, I'd make it better yet!"

Her great-aunt remembers when all the sand on the beach
Was hers, and all the foam-ruffled waves danced for her
Alone. There are times, she must admit, when she wishes
She could have that same kind of innocence back again.

The Underside of Stones

This stone came from Oregon's coast;
A small Henry Moore sculpture it is,
Hole like a window through which to see
A different world. Two smaller stones
Cling to the hollow, having clung
Through tides both ebb and flow,
Their bottoms serrated like teeth.

If you have ever walked upon a beach
Along the coast of Oregon, you know
Why this tenaciousness. No soft sand
Takes your footprint; it is one stone
After another, ranging from pebbles
To boulders—take care walking there.

Now, this one beckoned from a posted
Falling Rock Zone—serendipitous because
Its mica brightness beaconed out
From an otherwise indistinguishable
Heap. That it survived the rockfall
Is a wonderment. It flakes, you see,
Unlike the hardier specimens built up
From strata, visible layers of time.
But how can one resist it? It shines
So in the sunlight, and it fits just
Right into a jeans pocket to take home.
Set in the side garden, it need know
No more harsh traveling, and can endure.

Finally, my favorite stone. You see
This fish, its bony shape imprinted
Like a petroglyph? It tells us
In a literal translation that once,
Eons ago, where we stand was ocean,
Or glacier melt, or a great flood...
The underside is smooth as an egg,
Another sign that water has washed it.

I look at this fish fossil and think
How children form snow-angels,
Making their bid for immortality
(When this you see, remember me.)

But sun melts angels made of snow,
And stone let fall can shatter history.

Depth Perception

I never trust the shadows of the night
For what, in their dark velvet folds, may hide:
That thing not known, that does not hurt, but might.

My step is measured, tentative and light,
Exploring, inch by inch, what may betide
I never trust the shadows of the night.

There are such expectations to excite:
Mind's deep imaginings may still abide:
That thing unknown, that does not hurt, but might.

If I could mold my past, would I revise, rewrite,
Would I explore life at its ebb of tide?
I never trust the shadows of the night.

Such shapeless shades have power to affright;
My apprehension cannot be denied
Of things unknown, that do not hurt, but might.

My greatest fear is not to set foot right,
Discover, all unbidden, my dark side:
That thing unknown, that does not hurt, but might.
I never trust the shadows of the night.

Yard Sale

My neighbor, braver than I,
Is having a yard sale: to sell
Things that propel memories;
I blush and admit, I could not.

Things are so here and now,
Having survived then and when,
I simply cannot imagine parting
With what was the heart of that day.

Awful power is what *things* have:
They alone can summon memories
Even if unwanted, even less than
Happy, for often they are life.

If a hand-knit sweater, less skill
Than love, is offered for sale,
Its knitter long a granite stone,
Who can blame the happy buyer?

Small wavelets of pleasure abound
Here, where anything's adventure.
And I wish them well from my safe
Haven, resolved never to do the same.

X-Ray: The Interior Landscape

Here works the Ansel Adams of the bones.
He searches out the shadows of one's self
For truth: where hides the fracture, where the cells
Are merged into a mass of mystery.

Your bones and ligaments and tendons bared,
The smallest fissure shown as an abyss:
The plates remind of Adams' classic shot,
The Moon Above Yosemite, its planes of rock,
Of peaks and valleys almost skeletal.

Yet, having marveled, peering at the plates,
This patient sighs, the picture incomplete,
Deluded by a quest: to seek her soul!

The Last of the Summer Tomatoes

A straw-dry drought thatched the garden patch
All Summer anyway, but now, in Autumn, a gift
Of tomatoes the size of grapes, making us richer
Than rubies could have. They have such fanciful
Names: "Tiffany" for the little ones, "Best Boy"
For the ones bigger but nothing to boast about,
Not this year. Drought stunted all growth.

Still, in Autumn, we can turn the sprinkler on
And bathe the last of the Summer tomatoes in
A fine spray, more like morning dew, sparkling
In the sun's rays at the end of the day.

The water makes the little tomatoes glisten, jewels
Unknown to us before, all the more precious for
Being so few. And, what's more, the drops
Look the way we imagine their flesh to taste,
Bitten into right there, standing at garden's edge,
Juice dribbling down the chin. Joy needs no
apology.

Lost in Translation

I'm looking at the wishful window
Of my favorite used book store,
Wishing, indeed, that I had money—
Not a lot, just some not prioritized
To bills and other obvious obligations.

I have to tell myself the truth of things:
While I'd certainly love to take home
Half the display window, all I *should*
Buy is that handsome little edition
(Red cloth binding, (gilt and *guilt*)
On spine and edges of pages, delicious
As any offering in the next door deli,
None of which I can afford, either.)

Well, let's move on down the avenue,
Then, determined as I seem to be
To avoid the occasion of sin once again.

But wait! I just put hand in pocket,
Checking for some forgotten bus fare,
When I feel the crisp crackle of paper
Money, and withdraw hand to show
A five-dollar bill I didn't remember.
At the used book store, five will go a
Long way in paperbacks. But, in the
Case of the red cloth binding, a bit
Chancier. The little voice inside my
Head, the voice that keeps me solvent,
Says, "Get the cloth binding. It will
Last longer, and may even be worth
Something, someday." Lost in translation
Is the unspoken disclaimer that it's not
A first edition and so worth very little.

Meanwhile, the paperbacks' gaudy covers
Shine under cheap fluorescent tubes,
Their promise to take me away from
This blue Monday to sunnier climes
Implicit in any transaction for escape.

Two Canyons

Once, long ago, I lived there:
Concrete canyons rising steep
Beside the narrow city streets
Where, they said, the heart of
The metrosphere hummed bee-busy.

But no stars could be tracked
In that night sky – too many of
The bright lights competing for
Attention – not twinkling distant
But assaulting the senses boldly.

Now, I am home again, where, at
Dusk, ribbons of purple band sky;
Constellations are mapped against
The dark velvet of deepening night.
Coyotes, wolves, nightstalkers all.

Red rocks rise beside the arroyo,
Stone spires like cathedrals',
Reaching for Heaven, perhaps;
The arches of birch and aspen far
More to me than Gothic sanctuaries.

Old friends back there asked me
To come visit them soon again, not
Knowing (how could they?) how I
Miss my older friends, these vital
Mountains layered by geologic strata.

But they are just stones, after all;
Pebbles to boulders, only stones
Whose silence is forever.
I'm not so sure.

Pieces of the Mountain

I want no mountain summits set for me –
A tenderfoot, yes, even after years
Of watching mountains without climbing one...
Of seeing city canyons counterparts
Forever caught in architectural
Comparisons which flirt with heresy,
Perhaps, considering the Architect
Who was the maker of this Grand Design!

Along a gentle trail I gather stones
And hold one layered with strata made by time;
Another, egg-smooth, washed with water gone
For ages; and a fish-shape fossil stone.
These pieces of the mountain come to me,
This timid flatlander who calls a hill
A mountain – Smile-Alert for Westerners
Who never know the terror of a foot
Set wrong, a slip with nothing there to catch
The alien from another place in time.

Reflection

Where once a mirror hung upon this wall,
Now empty chasm yawns, awaiting hand
Of plasterer and painter to restore
The clean austerity of what was here,
But silvery reflection's lost its sheen.

I cannot catch a glimpse of self to see
If I may need to brush my windblown hair,
Or even reassure me I exist!

Did I, too, disappear when hammers struck
The wall down, taking with it my old image?

Some things will not bear thinking of too long,
For pondering is ponderous, as well.
I trust it was not vanity alone
That sent me on a mirror quest so soon.

Trail Ridge Vista

There are no softly-rounded edges;
This country asks no quarter, and gives none.
At timberline, the soil's unfriendly;
There's none to spare for Nature's gardening—
And yet you'll see the frailest flowers
Abloom wherever last year's seeds have blown.
Bare roots cling to the cloven rocks, here,
And trees grow one side only in this wind.
Still, they endure: they bend; submit; bow—
They green the grey, unyielding stone...and stay.

The Wind-Gardener

A wild flower is a weed become a friend,
The way one might describe, say, Queen Anne's Lace:
From wind-blown seeds come nosegays for the heart.
There's Indian Paintbrush, colors splashed across
A valley vista, there for all who dare
To climb that high to see, a live landscape.
There's Columbine, five petals porcelain-thin,
Translucent cup, transcendent bravery.
Withstanding all the weather's whims and winds.
The Sagebrush blooms and scents the arid air
With pungence all its own: desert perfume.
Above the timberline, a tiny star
Of white, as pure as hope, conquers the odds
Against it, digs in, clings to a short life
If that's what the gods send—who knows which way
The wind will blow next time, how far away?

Trout Hangout

Frying Pan River, Basalt, Colorado.

Under the wands of the green willow tree,
The river narrows here to calm stream
Tamed enough to tempt fishers of trout,
Who endure the water's all but frozen flow
Over expensively booted feet now numbed.
The trout though, thrive in such chill,
Their silvery skins like coats of mail
Protecting that sweet delicate flesh beneath.

Solitude and silence are other reasons
To wait with patience for revealing splash.
Ah, but splash reveals danger too,
To wilier trout, who plunge emerald depths
To bottom, pretending to be river stones
Of little interest to a greedy fisherman.
Where else, it might be fair to ask,
Can a man give the illusion of occupation
While doing absolutely nothing but waiting?

You could say, both creatures abide
In their truest element. I would.

Morning Sun on a Red-checked Tablecloth

Searching rays make sense of the table,
What is going to happen there and why:
It's hungry time, that's all: 7 a.m.
I could have slept later, but then this
Poem would not be even beginning.
You really have to be hungry
For it to matter very much at all.

Sunlight glints off sugar and creamer
Painted with ivy tendrils, old, very old.
They are fat little vessels, as if to warn
That eating too much from either fattens us,
As well. But we do not really care about
That, about getting fat, on such a morning.
There are leaves to be raked, and it's really
A Mister Rogers day in our neighborhood.

Sunbeams gleam across the table: striking
What may not really be silver (there is real
Silver hiding in tarnish-proof wraps, but it
Needs polishing. We do not polish silver
Before breakfast. We don't care quite that
Much, not before breakfast. Try us later.)

Like a searchlight, sun seeks out headlines
On the front page of the daily newspaper—
These are predictably grim, so let's go right
To the heart of the paper that matters: the not-
Always funny funny pages. Some of the clever
Comics are done by cartoonists with agendas.
Especially in an election year, Heaven knows.

What ever happened to jokes, do you suppose?
Did the great outside world take over this, our
Small and private corner of the planet, making
Everything a Very Serious Matter Needing Your
Immediate Attention. Never mind; there's plenty
Of need to go around. Meanwhile, you must make
A choice of marmalade or plum jam and try not
To feel guilty about enjoying the possibilities.

Terror for Breakfast

Propping the pristine paper against a pitcher,
I see the front-page photo, in mid-Winter grey
And grainy but for the swath of police tape
Spewing its yellow scream: DANGERDANGER
Where terrible acts broke midnight silence
Only eight hours before.
There is a depression
In the white, where some unlucky one, fallen,
Made a live snow-angel, hands outstretched
Forming wings, while pleading for his life.
So: no need for the crime-scene chalk outline
Marking where the latest bullet felled a boy
Not even yet a man.
My snug, small house is no fortress, its walls
Not impregnable, its silvery ribbons of security
Wired to alarms no guarantees.
On such a day as this
I wrap myself in mittens and muffler, not even
Looking at thermometers.
It suddenly seems unbearably cold out there.

Hot Pink

More red flowers bloom there
Than I have ever known—
Blood-flowers, some of them.

Heat rises in wavy spirals
From pitted flagstones,
Burnished pink by rain
Falling suddenly
As if a hand had let drop
A curtain of bright beads.

A little, mangy cur laps
At an iridescent puddle
In a frenzy before it evaporates
In this shimmering air,
Just as the painter
At his easel across the way
Frantically dabs and scrubs
From canvas to palette
And back again
Before it gets away from him.

Blossoms drop; new red blooms.

The Crafts of Art

Hints of and ways to show a newer, deeper layer of the puzzle...

Portals

Homage to Domenic Cretara and his door paintings.

DOOR OPENS [Speaker: man returning to boyhood home]

Let me in! Let me in!
There are locks but no doorknob
On this weathered, paneled entryway;
I note that even the brick is scumbled,
And the wooden pillars, imitations
Of far grander marble, Doric and Ionic –
Even they have come down in the world.
There's heavy traffic noise out here,
And even a cloud of carbon monoxide,
Thick as fog poisoning the heavy air.
You are my only chance to escape,
So how can you refuse me refuge?
Let me in! Oh, let me in! Let me...

DOOR CLOSES

Let me out! Let me out!
Within, my house is a mind museum
Or a mined museum, ready to implode.
That very chair is where I hid from all
Terrors of the day, shadows of the night.
The ottoman is where I had to bend me
Into an obedient shape for a whipping
From a belt with a big, bruising buckle.
It no longer matters if I was innocent—
It didn't hurt any the less. Now, out
The back door, I stumble through weeds
Untamed by that rusted rake by the door.

A long shadow casts itself upon the door,
Which has a doorknob to let one inside.
The long shadow is me, and I question
Who would want to come in here again?

Secrets of the Stone

Her hands are small but able, scarred
From many a random slip of chisel,
Many a gypsy chip of granite
Seen too late to duck, perceived
As motes in sunlit shafts of studio light.
Her eyes are bright as polished lapis,
One brow convex as a circumflex,
Arched in permanent surprise
(Another chip struck, another time).

A dangerous place, this, where vast
And unforgiving stones resist the sculptor,
Behaving like creatures from the wild
And she their tamer. She tells them
Truth, with every hammer blow she strikes:
She only wants to set their spirits free.
And if the spirit should take shape,
Some form not even she could hope for?
Then that is what she and the stone were
Born for, that and the path
That led them to each other.

Madame Greets Her New Class

How many has the mirror shimmered back
Across the years, caught in its silver view?
The seasons in Madame's own almanac
Are marked by "Swan" and "Nutcracker" anew.

Small duckling to be transformed into swan,
And tomboy leaps, to fairy tour jetes,
The air an element to glide upon.
Some will not know the magic, all their days,
But, now and then, a foot will arch just so—
A hand will reach for that elusive rose;
Together, notes and dancer seem to flow.
For this, she strikes her most majestic pose,
And motes of dust in sunlight shafts unseen,
The little ones are members of her court—
And she is once again the reigning queen.
From out the past, new dreams come to transport.

Riders of the Silver Screen

All Gene Autry had to do
Was twirl his lasso to ensnare
My prepubescent heart.
It helped, of course, to hear
The Sons of the Pioneers or such
Singing sadly but in harmony
About loneliness and lost loves.
Those horses, too sleek steeds
Always prettier than the sweet
But plainly-dressed schoolmarm
Who could not compete with
Silver-studded, handtooled
Leather costing more than her
Wedding dress, were she allowed
To wear one – which she never was.
The cowboy hero seemed always
Ready to get on his faithful horse
And ride off into the sunset.
Was she consoled by one final,
Wistful chorus of "Happy Trails to You"
Drifting into the desert distance?

Poetic Process

*Backstage: with any luck, the sounds of sawing
and hammering will not be heard out front...*

The Edible Past

Proust had the proper notion:
Place a taste on the tongue
And let it evoke as it will
Memory of another place,
Another time. Savor it to
Its fullest dimension. Most
Importantly, remember...

Surely, the child Marcel
Could have done better
Than a mere cookie that was
Not even quite sweet enough.

My personal Madeleine
Was a buttery cinnamon-
Sprinkled treat, just what
A Kewpie Doll child with
Dimples atop dimples needed.

It wouldn't work for me today:
All I could think of would be
Calories, forbidden calories,
And what fun, may I ask,
Is that? Ah, but there's the
Flaw: reminiscence is not
Always meant to be fun.

If you wish to recover memory,
Though, you must endure a bit
And swallow your former pride.
What says *It's all there*,
As if waiting to be rediscovered,
Like a familiar taste or scent?

Invoking the Muse

One fine and hopeful Spring day
While waiting for a bus downtown
I was approached by a graceful girl
Who said she was a Muse...it was
Easy to believe her since she wore
Diaphanous chiffon in early April,
Her hair in a classical Psyche knot.
She did not even shiver in the wind
That sweeps concrete canyons
Of city streets that time of year...she
Was radiant as any Maxfield Parrish
Nymph ever painted. How does one
Begin a conversation with a Muse?

I did not falter. "Please, oh please
Help me! Help me write a poem
Of such compelling, vivid beauty
That, no matter what comes after it,
Critics will point to my poem as
A standard of pure perfection."

She gazed at me in wonderment.
"Ohhhh," she said sadly. "Erato
Is *your* Muse. I'm Thalia, and
I don't *do* poetry." Noting my
Look of disappointed rejection –
A frequent expression of mine –
She added, "It's not my job!"
"Well, then," I countered, "The
Least you can do is a-Muse me!"

Dialogue

C'MON, get up!
Let's go!

That's my Muse
Talking. She can
Be quite annoying.

Let's move! You
Think you have
All day? I'm waiting
Here. But not forever.

My Muse turned up one
Day when I was eight
Years old, in 3rd grade.
She helped me write my
First poem and earned
Me a dollar, my first
Dollar, too.

If you're grateful, you
Have a funny way of
Showing it. Don't try
To ignore me. Let's
Get to work.

I'm tired, I try to tell
Her. I must have done
Hundreds of poems by
Now. Isn't that enough?

No, it's never enough.

Remembering Emily

Emily Dickinson, 1830-1886

The quiet country churchyard still
Recalls the Belle of Amherst well,
And ivy greening her small bed
May weave a wreath around her head.

The songs of lark and mockingbird
Might be the same sounds she once heard
A hundred years ago and more,
Reprising like a sweet encore.

On Sundays long ago, she strolled
These grassy pathways here and told
Her spirit-visions to no one,
As silent as a cloistered nun.

Demure she was, dressed all in white,
An unimposing figure slight
As any cygnet's quill she penned
Her lines with, even to the end.

At dusk, when evening shadows fall,
The bell for Vespers sounds its call.
Thus it may happen: some shall see
The wraith of 1883.

As gauzy as sheer-winged moth
A spectre not of flesh and cloth,
But spirit, rises from her rest
Miss Dickinson to manifest.

The Reluctant Sonnet

With what a hammering of iambic feet
The rhythms, curled and coiled, lie supine now;
Conforming to that most insistent beat
The muse to rigid discipline must bow.
Suppose I long to catch a butterfly?
Too late! Too bad, it's slipped the sonnet's net.
No antic dance can be done justice by
This stiff and stately two-step, nor will let
The ear be too surprised by what it hears.
All music, forced in such a vise of mold
Becomes a vice entire, nor yet endears
Itself. Must it be prized for being old?

O sonneteers, you anvil hammerers:
Have mercy on reluctant stammerers!

Villainous Villanelle

The villanelle is villainous, I fear,
Though musical and lilting in its song,
And charming though its antics may appear.

These antics are iambics that ensphere
The fiendish form, and yet must not ding-dong;
The villanelle is villainous, I fear.

I rail against the fate that puts me here,
Mere poet wishing to put no foot wrong,
And charming though its antics may appear.

I pray your kind indulgence if I veer
From charted challenge which I meet headlong:
The villanelle is villainous, I fear.

I try not to become too cavalier
By patching up my verse with a diphthong,
As charming as its antics may appear.

I think, perhaps, I am a sonneteer,
Not meant to vie with villanelle too long.
Though musical and lilting in its song,
And charming though its antics may appear.

Replacement Poem

You should have seen the one that got away!
It shone and shimmered like a silver trout,
A wily one, eluding capture's hook,
Too slippery to catch, too quick for prey.

Find me another metaphor to play
A different metric line, surprisingly
Like a cello in a string quartet, perhaps,
That resonates with newer words to say.

Or, let a dancer's dazzling taps display
A syncopated rhythm all their own,
Yet echoed by a drummer in the pit,
And never danced again in this same way.

I want that poem, the one that got away;
I visualize it drifting down the stream
Of consciousness, and always just beyond
My reach: imagination's holiday.

Caging the Wild Words

Safaris made with camera or gun
May well be less intrepid, in the end.
This is the shyest beast of all: the one
Assiduously sought: the Word which, penned,
Will captivate, with poetry so sweet
That it would lure still more elusive Words
To follow, to submit to metric beat,
And sing, full-throated, as do all caged birds.
Safari's end in sight, let's celebrate
Not victories, brief triumphs of the mind,
But all our explorations validate
According to what we may, delving, find.

The majesty of every untamed beast...
The missing trophy when the hunt has ceased.

Upon a Tranquil Bed

It is too quiet here.
I think that I could hear
The smallest sound, the stop
And start of breath; the drop
Of summer rain from trees
To ground; the slightest breeze
That bends tall grass in arcs
Of artistry; the lark's
Sweet murmur in its throat—
Oh, mark its softest note!
I sought but peace, an end
Ungained by my own hand,
Which has so finally
Committed me to lie
With my tormented head
Upon a tranquil bed.

It is forever silent in the deep abyss of Hell
For one whose ears, assailed by quiet, must yet yearn
For what can never be: the swift, complete return
Of nagging, little sounds he once had rued to know so well.

Satire, Very Mild

*Urging a return from delusions of immortality to the
nub of what makes a poem...*

At the Altar of Ab(so)lution

Good morning, Mirror. I see you've lost
A little of your silver, as I have gained
More of mine. This daily inspection
Keeps us both in balance, perhaps.

I wash this same face today
As yesterday and tomorrow
Will see me: tired from restless
Sleep: wrestling with worries
That are no less distressing
Because I know they are not
Worth fretting over, rationally.
Ah, but who can be that rational
In the throes of the 3 a.m. blues?

I will not smile until I brush
My teeth, if you've no objection.
Have you noticed, Mirror, how
We penitents who face you daily
Seem to want to look our best,
Especially when we may have
Done our worst, or close enough
Not to make any difference?

Do we delude ourselves: if we but
Wash and brush we can regain
Some semblance of lost youth,
Some reflected ghost of beauty?

Is it my penance to polish you,
Mirror? How can I, when you
Would see too clearly
What I have become!

Penitential

I may never write again.

I am a writer without a pen.
My faithful old Parker which
I stoked with ink refills
To feed its insatiable hunger;
Its dignified casing I polished
—I have to say—with patient
Pride; its silver and gold nib—
All of that is gone, gone, gone.

I may never write again.

Never mind this keyboard I tap
Relentlessly every day. Every
Word is better if first written
By hand with a Parker pen.
Verse flows from its nib as if my
Poetry too were silver and gold.
That this is not so, I know.
But the illusion has such power!

I may never write again.

Where could the essential pen
Have gone? The penitential poet
Pats pockets and purses, all hope
Eroding with each futile failure.

Do I say with regret or relief:
I may never write again?

A Political Commentator Reviews the Autumn Situation

It was revealed to this observer by a trusted source
That Autumn will officially return this Friday next,
Confirming our prediction that September twenty-first
Would mark the Fall's inaugural: at least, throughout the North.
The South may be a little slower in acknowledging
Its leadership, but Autumn has some strong supporters there.

The implications of this circumstance are several:
An early frost is possible, but Indian Summer may
Retain its hold, although the likelihood of this is small.

It is a certainty that we shall see the hills in plaid again,
And drink of amber cider, and grow hoarse at football games,
And smile at children scuffling feet through gutters thick with
leaves
Unconscious that they tread on tiny corpses every step.

Of all the Big Four Seasons, Autumn is dependable
As to behavior more than any other. Even Spring,
Which follows Winter, breaks its promises repeatedly—
Rebirth, a new beginning, although they are desirable,
Are unattainable. No idealistic season, this.
We feel our confidence is not misplaced in stating that
This timely change should be of general benefit to all.

Baiting a Bookworm

Had I been asked to go with **Hemingway**
To Africa or Spain, I would have sighed
Regretfully, "Perhaps some other day..."
Returning to his **book,** safe by my side.

Had **Scott FitzG.** invited me to dine,
In charming phrases come from long ago,
I would remember that for him the wine
Became the meal and, sadly, would say, "No."
(Adventure thrives in *Tender Is the Night.*)

Miss Dickinson, dear **Emily,** had she
But wondered timidly if I just might
Accept her invitation to high tea. . .
I would put down my book, I must confess,
At last, with all my heart, I would say, "YES!"

The Ballad of Willie Nelson's Bandanna

Oh, listen to the story of good ol' Willie Nelson
And his love for the pinto bean—
Willie liked his chili served up hot and wholesome,
Said it made him feel lean and mean!

Across this great nation, from Frisco to Philly,
When Willie was travelin' on tour,
He searched in vain for The Perfect Bowl of Chili
Fabled in legend and lore.

One fateful night in Summer Willie hankered for chili
Wonderin' where he would find the best?
He met up with a cute and friendly-lookin' filly,
And put that little gal to the test!

"Can you make a pot o' chili, filly mine, filly mine?"
So warbled hungry Willie...
She replied with some pride that her chili was "divine",
She made it with piccalilli!

Willie thought that filly was just too darn silly
To trust with his favorite dish—
So he drove to a diner, speeding willy-nilly,
And told the cook his dearest wish.

"Cook me up some chili, you ol' hillbilly,
Cook it up spicy and hot!"
That cook got busy at his greased-up grill, he
Knew Willie would eat a lot.

Willie took one bite and grinned with delight—
This chili was heavenly manna,
Pleased and appeased Willie's huge appetite—
As a napkin, he used his bandanna.

Fear of Phobias

My phobias are copious, I fear.
When flying, I assume the end is near
If "unexpected turbulence" is met,
And tend to escalate from prayer to fret.

It's not the speed and altitude so much,
As hoping Captain has not lost his touch.
It's not when I am airborne I lose hope,
As when we hover over mountain slopes.

The jagged rockface reaches like Kong's hand,
And turns me into an analysand.
If we are set down gently, how prosaic
Anxiety becomes—formulaic.

Now back on *terra firma*, I deplore
My every shudder uncontrolled, before
"Nothing to fear but fear itself," I hear,
And hope whoever said it was sincere.

Philosophical Differences

You can't keep everything, you know.
Of course not. Where would you put it?
— Magnet message

My bright white Frigidaire, Model FRT18FS5A,
Is a true magnetic field for aphorisms,
Political potshots, declarations of love,
Yet remains pure and impartial.
Do not sully its white with scandal.
It is not prying or prurient. It remains
As calm as a dulcet dove, always and ever.

Anything that could be printed on a magnet 2x3
Has an egalitarian place on the fridge.

"The best is yet to be!" says Browning,
Despite all evidence to the contrary.
But a curmudgeon of the same vintage
Snarls with impunity, "Hah!" His
Brevity must be respected, even though
You may not wish to endorse his P.O.V.

"Life is something to do when you can't get to sleep,"
says Fran Lebowitz. Woody Allen declares,
"It's not that I'm afraid to die; I just don't want
To be there when it actually happens."

All of this becomes a controversy,
Or, even worse, a cacophony of views.

But, given the fact that the refrigerator
Is what it is, the Frigidaire keeps its cool.

Pencil Sketch

I wish I could remember what it was
That set my heart to racing when we met,
So long ago your cheeks wore faint peach fuzz.

The bees grew sleepy and forgot to buzz;
The garden was too fecund to forget!
I wish I could remember what it was

That set my heart to racing when we met.
But memory does not click, or it does,
And I cannot remember what it was.

So soon there was a we and then an *us*,
Although the color of your eyes I knew not yet,
And still I cannot remember what it was.

Our days seemed then to rush without pause,
But why I seem determined to forget,
And wish I could remember what it was

That set my heart to racing when we met,
You were a quick one with a kiss, a buss
Upon the brow, all slick with Summer sweat
I hoped you would not notice, or forget
Midsummer's messy magic, you the cause
That set my heart to racing when we met.

The Passionate Shepherdess Regrets She Must Decline

"Come live with me and be my love,
And we will all the pleasures prove"
The Passionate Shepherd to His Love - Christopher Marlowe 1564-1593

It pains me to express reluctance now
When you have bared your heart, and promised how
Ideal, idyllic our joined lives would be-
If only I loved you as you love me.

But oh! My sweet adoring rustic swain,
My love is not enough to serve for twain;
I would be free of all love's subtle chains,
To wander with my flock o'er hills and plains,

To sip from silver streams; to find a bed
In any mossy hollow; rest my head
And watch the drama of the changing sky—
These pleasures are enough for such as I.

Pray find yourself another likely lass,
And have your little dalliance on the grass,
But let me go, and I will think of you—
Whenever I have nothing else to do!

Slither

It was only an apple, said the snake,
Rather defensively. I didn't mean
Any harm. Just following orders,
Was all. You have no idea where my
Allegiance lies, or what happens if I
Try to shift it.

It was a pretty, shiny red apple; from
Its round contours you could tell how
Juicy it would be to bite into. Ssso good!

Eve was such a girl, shining with innocence,
Something had to be done about *that*. Think
Of a garden garlanded with fragrant flowers,
And one tree casting long shadows over all.
This was my tree, the Tree of Knowledge.
I just wanted to share it with the pretty Eve.

One bite, one instant, and it was too late
To stop the sudden sensation of shame.
Eve knew for the first time she was naked,
And tried to cover herself with any/every
Growing thing she could rip by its roots
In her garden until all around her lay
Torn remnants and shreds of innocence.

Ssso sssad, hissed the snake insincerely,
But with every appearance of contrition.
You must know how dull it would be,
Except for me.

A Shopping Mall-Shaped Poem

I only went there for a spool of thread,
A means to mend my life,
To make myself presentable again.
But then I was assaulted on all sides
By new appeals:
To make you thinner, *The Spa!*
To make you unforgettable, *Casbah Cologne!*
To make you over...to make you...
As if, perhaps, I had
Not yet been born?
The jeweler's window dazzled;
The music shop played antidotes
To the blandest tunes in the world
Permeating the arcade,
Sarabandes of sweetness
As cloying as incense.
Aromas of indulgences as yet untapped.
Did I want popcorn in a dozen tastes?
Or else a double-chocolate cone?
A dozen roses plastic-wrapped
And drooping on their stems
Before they even left the shop?
No, none of these, together or alone,
Would be my choice,
If choose I could!
I came out into the brightness,
Into the sun again,
Clutching just one small paper bag.

I only went there, as I said,
To buy a spool of thread.

The Meek Shall Inherit the Earth...

If that's OK with the rest of you.

When I consider how my mild assent
Just echoes everybody's sentiment,
I must confess I cannot see quite how
(Since nobody has listened to me up to now)
My friends and I shall be in charge of all,
Regardless of our voices, soft and small
And unaccustomed to a large command—
This frightening prospect I can't understand!

The Wound and the Knife

"You cut me!" said the wound, gaping.
"Sorry, but I felt nothing at all," said the knife.

"I tasted blood," said the mouth.
"I had to suck the wound. Scary."
"Never been scared," said the knife.

"I hurt; don't you care?" said the wound.
"The business of knives is merely cutting,
Not caring what they cut," said the knife.

"But YOU did it!" accused the wound.
"No more than I would slice a peach,
Or slit open a letter," said the knife.

"I am only a tool," said the knife.
"You will have to look elsewhere
To fix your blame," said the knife.

"I need help now!" screamed the wound.
"I can be mended to meet tomorrow."
"*Good luck,*" said the knife. "There are
A lot of knives out there…just waiting."

After the Poetry Reading

These are the true aficionados:
They trek up to the lectern smiling
Improbable smiles (no comic moments
In the reading); these are appeasement smiles.

They don't know what to say.
It's almost as if they had wandered
Into the wrong funeral parlor
Not knowing either the celebrants
Or the guests, having to say something
Comforting and blurting out, "Lovely!
Simply lovely!"

The poet looks startled at hearing this much
Approval and wishes to ask the speaker for a blurb
To go on the jacket of the next book. But that would
Not be seemly. Bad enough to have a small, discreet
Pile of books for sale. Make that a small, disheartening
Pile of books.

The evening's event planner beams at the straggling
Members of the audience, ragged souls in need of mending,
Perhaps, but nonetheless the budget crunch—lights blink on
And off, in case reminders are necessary. At last, all
But poet and event planner are gone. The poet shakes
A hand, not caring at all whose hand it may be,
Breathes a soft "thanks so much"—the voice is the first
Thing to go after poetry readings—and exits by electric eye
Controls at the door. "Swish!" is all the door has to say.

Travel

Someplace never tested or tried before, all familiar landmarks missing—ah, but how tempting…

Luckpiece for a Traveler

A Zuni fetish carver named "Snowhawk"
Made this powerful small malachite bear,
Polished him to a mirror of your soul.
His eyes are turquoise blue, to guide you
On your journey and bring you back to me.

The bear has a prayer-bundle on his back,
Unspoken half-hopes that death in the street
Go unavailing, that you may go unvaporized
In traversing the seemingly endless skies.

You do not believe as "Snowhawk" does;
You do not even believe in how I pray—
But, just in case: wear this bear, anyway.
Indulge my superstition, if that's what you
Think it is; borrow my faith, if that's simpler.

Go now, go quickly, so that I can stand it:
That empty place where you should be.

My Address Book as History

Every time I pick it up, I sigh.
Its once-elegant cover is faded;
Its slim contours bulging with
Oddly-shaped inserts, balancing
Perhaps the enormity of X-ings
Denoting deaths, lost-track-ofs,
And other admissions of defeat.
Some entries have four or more
Changes of address—and still
I pursue them to other places,
Unwilling to let them disappear.

Sometimes I note I haven't been
To their newly-adopted country,
But can certainly imagine them
There, tasting the food, red wine
Decorating their table like flowers.

I could not give up this otherness
For anything. Put that book back!
Don't even *think* of throwing it away.

The Lamp-Lit Windows

Seen from a passing train,
A hundred miles since tree,
Or creature, or shabby shack
Broke flat horizon line,
Suddenly a wayside cabin
Becomes an architecture
For the mind's imaginings.

Warm and welcoming yellow
Glow the windows at just-dusk,
The time of day the traveler
Most longs for such a haven.

The train known as The Zephyr
Races on, its own wheel-wind
Bending prairie grasses low.

Encapsulated in the dining car,
A well-fed man sighs and pays
His check, longing for a place
And time he never knew
Except for that brief passing view.

Home, say the lamp-lit windows
To the heart of the romantic;
Come back, the train wheels whisper,
Before becoming *Clickety-clack.*

This Way to Baggage Claim→ →

After a Red Alert.

Why would any of us ever
Want to claim this baggage?
Didn't a random check reveal
Depths of anxiety at its vitals,
Waiting to spring like some
Small stowaway of an animal,
Coiled, wound tight, but hoping
Not to be seen, or, if seen, not
To be noticed, or, if noticed,
Not, at least, to be remembered.

It is not dignified, this fear so
Near the surface—yet here it is,
And here it seems to be staying.

There are remedies, diversions
Like prayer, but I worry lest He
May be suffering Deity Overload.
Like music, if it strikes the right
Note; no discordant innovations
For now. (Bartok might be jailed
For disturbing the peace.) Ask: is
There peace left to be disturbed?

Carousel 19 lets go like a rodeo
Chute disparate shapes and sizes
Of bags galumping in a circle,
Wrestled off the conveyor like
The Stock Show's bawly calves,
And just as resistant to handling.

Who among us does not long now
To be going home, bearing with us
Trophies of travel, tall tales to tell?

The Harbor at Juneau

Down by the piers, the ships pull into dock,
Gulls circling, searching, swoop with haunting cry—
And time means tide, not told by any clock,
But by the phases of the opal moon.

The queenly cruise ships, graceful, white as swans,
And sailing ships, must tuck and fold their wings
As sunset turns the channel to deep bronze,
And quiet fogs the harbor for the night.

Before first sun, the great swan-ships are gone,
Changed to toy boats on far horizon's line,
And tiny tugboats pull big barges on
Down toward Seattle, where they load again.

And, meanwhile, trawlers bring in their first catch—
Are greeted raucously by gulls once more;
The city's picnic-basket is the hatch:
Ten thousand meals are made of this cargo.

The land and water meld, down by the piers,
The waterfront a mix of rush and noise,
And never quite what it sometimes appears:
Tall tales from travelers; gossip from the gulls.

Ghost Town Near Red Mountain

Dust devils.
Trust me:
That's just
Stray winds
That mime riderless
Horses' hooves
Down old Main Street.

Isn't it?

And only random winds
Again that
Fill the bellows
Of the church
Organ, playing
Half-forgotten
Hymns by rote.

Trust me.

For who could
Pull the ragged rope
That makes the bell
Of the old schoolhouse
Ring out again, so pure and clear
In this deserted
Valley air?

<u>Of course, we are alone!</u>
(At least, I trust we are...)

On Finding a Postcard from Hawaii in the Mail One Bleak February Day

Just look! How white the Kohana Coast beach sand;
How blue the skies without a cloud to mar their vista;
How bright the ruffled red flowers to enhance the hula!

That's where my friends are, and I wish them joy of it.
Who could have guessed my paltry Summer
souvenirs
Of Atlantic seaboard: sand poured out from
Ragged beach shoes would seem so long ago?

Crunch!

Your future lies in the fate of this cookie.
— Fortune cookie *message*

Discovering this dire pronouncement,
Fragilely sheathed in pastry crescent,
I naturally took all precautions:
Wrapped the harbinger in oceans
Of cotton from blue box with red cross,
Guarding against the sudden loss
Of rowdy health and garrulous speech,
Wanting no misfortune to teach
What might be learned from sharp adversity
(Dropping out of <u>that</u> university),
And one day woke to a grey and grim sky,
Took my bearings, heaved a great sigh.
Acknowledging here it was at last:
Not to be missed, the final bombast...
Please, don't wait up—I may be <u>very</u> late.
I am going out to find my fate.

Far off, the distant cannon rumbles;
Someone was hungry, the cookie crumbles.

Travelogue: A Country Called Time

If tutored by the ticking tongues of clocks
Or coached by sibilant calendar leaves
To nudge us from a fussy prompter's box,
We might well learn the language, but reprieves
For impulses – blithe byways – are unknown.
One must, I think, abjure the traveler's vice:
To see and smell and taste the texture here,
And never read the guidebook over twice,
Nor let familiar songs seduce the ear
Nor any wish for dalliance ever own.

The arbitrary architecture here
Is structured elements with terraces –
Baroque in the beginning, now austere:
The curled Corinthian embarrasses;
Compatible is Doric's cubic square,
But old Ionic's scrolls to dust consigned.
So let the traveler's wayward foot beware
What he with serendipity might find.
A fine place for a visit – rankling rare –
It's only living there I cannot bear.

Somewhere South of Serendipity

It shames me, how easily I forget
The endless beauty of the sea
When I return home to mountains,
Mountains which I also try to love.

I've just come back from sand and sea,
The gulls' shrill cries still on my mind,
Almost painful assault on visitors' ears
It seemed, but the locals smiling wryly
With disdain at my surprised reaction.
(Too long, too long, I've been away.)

"But I was born here!" I want to declare.
They would not have it so. I was born
In a city hospital a hundred miles North,
Having nothing to do with sea and sand
And the humiliating disregard of gulls.

At the ruffles of water's foamy edge,
I furtively wash shells to take home,
My only souvenirs, or so I like to think:
But, opening my carryon bag at home,
I shake sand from two thousand miles
Away out of my bedraggled beach shoes.
Part of me, true, wants to keep it in a jar
Labeled with "Summer, 2004"—but no,
I am not whimsical enough for that. Nobody,
Not even the fiercest lover, can put Summer
In a labeled jar and hope to find it again.

Music Over Water

A hundred blue-water miles or so
North of Bergen, the coastal steamer
Weighs anchor for a Port of Call:
Thirty minutes docked for unloading
Supplies and mail; passengers let go
To follow in the wake of Eric Clapton,
Headlining a jazz concert in this town,
Small enough that the fans outnumber
Population three-to-one. Nobody minds
The crowded square, being jostled just
The price of admission, glad to be there.

Staying aboard, I ask our purser how far
The *Polarlys* has traveled that day. He
Speaks nautically and in Norwegian;
I lumber along in crash-course language,
Hoping we can reach each other somehow.

It doesn't take long; music floats to us,
Bursts like fireworks over ship's bow,
Wind whipping our flags: syncopation.
We smile in accord, loving every note.

At last the great bellow of the ship's horn,
Warning all roaming passengers back
For departure. Dockside diminishes as
We pull away, heading for another port,
One that's big enough for a name on the
Map. "What was the name of the first
Town?" "Eric Clapton's town, that's all
I know!" *Or care,* is the implied reply.

Time Flies

My old watch has wandered away, perhaps
In a bin at the Buffalo airport
In proximity to a passenger
Who oozed First Class ambience, luxury
Undreamed of by my basic old timepiece.

I recently upgraded its wristband
To sleek, seductive eelskin as reward
For all its years of service, keeping track
Of my events, both large and small, each day.

This may have been indulgent, I see now,
And may have made the watch forget its start
In life, a humble start, indeed: a store
With dozens just like it, all one low price.

Its accidental owner now reflects:
"Where did I buy this watch with eelskin strap?
It's old. It must have been when I was young
And hadn't much money yet, so long ago."
(Complacent smile, for now he has it all.)

He has it all, including my prized watch,
Which rather worries me, for I don't even know
Where they may have landed, what new time zone
Will govern every tick it registers—
Will it forgive me and my careless love?

Bridge to Concourse A

DIAlog after the 2006 Blizzard. DIA is Denver International Airport.

It was as if a wild animal had broken out
Of the zoo: the wind, the ceaseless snow.

Voices of four thousand passengers
Pacing the terminal like caged animals
It was too dangerous to set free rose in
Pitch, becoming a communal howl.

Angered and hungry not only for food
But for answers to queries like these:
      "When?"
      "Where?"
      "Who?"
      "Why me?"
      "Why not me?"

Airline agents' faces smooth as angels'
Carved from mortuary marble, at first.
After six hours, eight, ten they changed.
Voices from behind the ticketing counter
Went from reasonable, soothing low to
High-pitched exasperation, that high C
Few ever reach or hold with success.

Lengthening shadows stretch across
Those creamy peaks of tented roof,
Meant to remind us of mountains,
Seem vulnerable beyond imagining.
What will we do if snow seeps through?
Where will we find a space for sleep?
Who will we find whom we can trust
To sit next to, while sleep seeps in
Like a thief who didn't get his job
Description right: stealing memory
Of this harried, hurried day, not
Trophies he could sell, but who
Would buy?

Eye of the Quilter

Airborne, as new patterns
Sometimes seem, to her,
The quilter's eye scans
Disappearing landscape
From Seat 12C, Flight 203,
Leaving Earth for clouds
That may be the suburbs
Of Heaven, for all we know.
She rather hopes so, but for
Now she will do a new quilt
With squares like farmland,
The silver mirrors of lakes
And ponds reflecting those
Same clouds beyond her window
At 20,000 feet and climbing.

She must green the rolling hills
Her eye caught. #203 ascending,
And make blue the dome of sky
That blesses all with rainbow-span.

Homeward-bound, she sees her
Self in her mind's imaginings,
Arranging, rearranging until
Order is at last achieved, again.
People who ask her, "Why quilt?"
She regards as civilians, outside
The ranks of quiltmakers who
Never need to ask, who rule by
Right of skill and silver needles
A perfect world stitched together
With thread so strong no piece
Can detach, harmoniously whole.

Misdirection

Is what magicians call it:
(*Nothing up my sleeve,*
Nothing but empty hands)

It's a poem gone astray,
Like a letter written, mailed,
Yet never seen again; like the
Air stirred by hummingbird's
Wings, too small to be noticed
By most of the rest of the world.

If it were more like a bird,
This small poem could flit
From branch to branch—
And hardly mark the shift
That momentarily changes
The shape and structure
Of its chosen tree, as if a
Sudden gust of wind had
Altered the landscape—
But only for the moment,
For as long as it would take
For a click of camera shutter;
Just one—hear it, and go on.

But what of the magician's props?
You remember that shimmer
Of silken scarf of many hues,
That slipped out of the sleeve
Sworn to hold nothing at all.
Sheer serendipity, surely,
To have a poem emerge like
That, all light and gauzy color.
Could we try that again?
This time, I promise to watch
More closely, like a hunting dog
Poised to point the prize.

At the Mendenhall Glacier, Alaska

Cathedrals made of glass might look like this,
With ancient ice turned blue as heaven's hue—
That being how the eye reads prism's gleam.
Low parapets wall off a deep abyss
To make more sure a climber's cleated shoe,
Aware that things are never what they seem.
If we could stand and stare, wide-eyed but still,
(The glacier is forever; only we
Remain ephemeral; it does not change)
We soon would see the glacier moves to fill
One part of Nature's vacuum, steadily,
And makes familiar what before was strange.

Colossus formed of crystals, one by one,
Bedazzles in the early Northern sun.

Portraits

Putting all things into perspective...

Did Anyone See the Girl I Thought Was Me?

She was here a little while ago.
Did you see her hair, the color
Of an autumn leaf and she, too,
Like a leaf blown here and there
By every chance wind passing by?

Did you hear her laugh, turning
So quickly into a wistful sigh?
I think she may have left when she
Was challenged by an older woman:
"If you aren't careful, you will
End up just like me. You'll see."

I think the girl ran after her
Right then, calling out: "Wait,
Oh, wait for me: I need to know!"

Someone saw the girl dancing,
But that was before the encounter
With that which claimed to be real
Life. You don't recall? I under-
Stand—so many wind-buffeted leaves,
And new ones unfold every season.

Portrait

She is only waiting.
She is accidentally
The cold room's sudden warmth.
Her hair is shock above
The imposed decorum
Of all dark-blue dresses,
As yellow tulips that
Defy an ugly vase
To defeat their vibrance.
She would splinter mirrors
If they were cursed to hold
Her warmth in constant cold.

The Sundown Singer

Comes now the sundown singer,
In need of love as much as food!
No need to coax him – linger
He will, and tell tall tales, not truth.
He knows no tongue but fancy,
And money has he none at all –
Sung stories are his currency,
Their language strange; their power raw.
Yes, feed the wandering minstrel,
And mend his tattered patches well.
Yet think him not a wastrel
Who with his music spins a spell.
No need to praise his singing –
He knows if you heard him true.
His notes are blackbirds winging
Up high, away, and out of view.
You ask yourself, "Was he here?"
Or were you, for a little while,
Transported by his charming air
To some forbidden, foreign soil?

The Woman Who Was Not All There

They said of her: she never combed her hair;
It haloed wildly her ethereal face;
She gardened, sometimes, by the silvery moon;
Her housekeeping was ever in disgrace.

They said of her: she just was "not all there"—
Her grasp of social graces was not great;
She said, "Good morning" in the afternoon;
She never seemed to notice what she ate.

And true it was, she had some missing parts:
She lacked vindictive gossip, for a start;
And harbored neither malice nor revenge,
But ended every day with a light heart.

The Woman Who Was Not All There perhaps
Had found a secret those of us who <u>were</u>
(All There, that is) had overlooked, by chance.
Life cannot measured be by caliper!

Old Pawn Bracelet

It has that soft patina of old silver,
Much prized, much polished, worn
Sunrise to sunset, work to dancing.
Never taken off until a leaden day
Of too much hunger and no money.

You can see: the wrist that wore it
Had once been young and rounded,
But thinned by too many hard years;
There are faint lines in the silver
From bending it smaller and smaller.

Who was she, the old Zuni woman?
The rightful owner of this silver prize,
Her spirit still so strong I even hesitate
To pay the price and claim it for my own.
Somewhere, *she* knows it is *hers,* always.

Hopper's Houses

"The answer is on the canvas!"
Edward Hopper to those who asked, "What does it mean?"

Cape Cod Morning. The tawny-haired woman
Looks anxiously out her front window
Assessing the *strength* of early-morning sun:
Will it last long enough to dry her weekly wash?
Will the salty air a chance gust blows there
Make pillowcases billow like a small boat's sails?
If sun burns off fog, can she still hear the foghorns?
She loves the foghorns; they seek something, as she does.

Cape Cod Afternoon. Half in light, half in shadow,
At four o'clock the house shows a closed door;
Windows a blank stare with no figure behind them;
Even the dog is unseen, napping perhaps
In some cool, mysterious place his humans
Would not think to look so cannot disturb him.
Soon the kitchen will send out succulent signals
That dinner is in the works—the dog will return.

Cape Cod Evening. Behind the house, the woods
Form a dusky blue shade. Late afterglow strikes
The front of the house, turning the white paint
Shrill as a gull's cry. It is after dinner now;
The tawny-haired woman has donned a fresh blue dress
For her man's homecoming. He has shed city clothes
To play with his pet collie whose coat is a painterly
Echo of the woman's hair—no accident, you may be sure.
But the dog's focus is drawn away by a bird's cry—
Not one of the beings in the scene relates to another.

Hopper's houses are made of more than wood and stone;
Sometimes they wear human guise, or animal—

But always and ever they are alone.

The Artist's Wife

For Jo Hopper, eclipsed by the more famous Edward.

You had visions of your own,
Abstract swatches of color
Swirling inside your bright head,
That tawny-haired model we saw
On so many of his canvas squares.
One wonders how you felt, giving
Up your time at the easel for his,
Holding a pose that must have
Been painful to stiffening limbs
Over the span of relentless years.

You had no child except for him:
The artist who must be cosseted
And soothed, yet who comforted you
When your work went unrecognized?

I wish I could have watched you then,
Making your own world on the easel,
Blissfully lost until the cry: "Jo! Come!"
Interrupted once again. Edward needed—
And his needs were always met; yours,
Of course, could always wait—until
It was too late. The tyranny of time!

He left two thousand paintings when
Time ran out for him. You had a year
To be yourself, to be Josephine at last!

But bitter was the paradox! At eighty,
Your long-fingered hands, an artist's,
Were too stiff to hold a brush. Visions
Were locked within your ivory skull,
Known only to God, who gifted you.

Protective Armor

Shimmer
   Shiver
      Glitter
         Gleam

Frail armature,
Shoulderblades like
Sparrow wings,
Dressed in satin
Of a silver sheen,
Clothes the singer
At the last show
On Saturday night
Must have borrowed.
Only her song tells
It true: Her heart
Wears a ragged coat,
No proof against the cold.

All I Wanted Was a Doll

After a painting by Josef Head.

None too willing
Is she to give
Her flower-stalk waist to the making
Of a child; nor almond-tipped hands
To dig in dirt, make clean the house,
Bake the loaf for her love's waking;
None too willing
Is she to live.

It is enough to be,
She tells the green bird
Tied to a shortening leash;
She speaks her futile word,
Me, her only guarantee
On this fragile day
In an orange-sunned May
Of perpetually rosy flesh,
Always-shining hair,
Upon a canvas square.

John Donne at Dawn

Upon a country road in Oregon,
Two jubilant joggers meet in chill-grey dawn;
The fog enwraps them like their hooded shirts;
Beneath their urgent feet, sprayed water spurts.

Adidas pounding out a metric beat,
Iambic rhythms rise and fall, repeat.
Obscured by mist, the ghost of old John Donne
Counts cadence as they run in unison.

"GO and CATCH a falling star...
Tell me where all past years are!"

Still chasing stars in 1631,
The brightest in the firmament was Donne.
A star fell, surely, when his own light dimmed.
Three centuries are gone, his lines still hymned
By this unlikely pair with few past years;
The sounding of their feet applauds, reveres.

These two are met upon a winding road,
And none can say what may their future bode.

"MUST to THY motions lovers' seasons run?"
Asked John Donne when he saw the rising sun.

I ask John Donne, in Heaven's high estate,
To plead for these two, running, a kind fate.
May roads be ever smooth beneath their feet,
And hills crest gently as their runs complete!

Feathers from Stone

Gary Eagle Plume sculpts a warrior chieftain.

Inside the rock,
Inside the roughness
Waits the sleek skin
Polished and proud
Over sharp cheekbones
Over taut throat muscles
Stretched over bow-arm.

This I will find
For I know it is there
Tap-tap the echo
Of my seeking chisel
Sharp like the drumbeat
Louder and louder
Closer and closer.

The drums for war
A giant's heartbeat
An angry giant, heedless
Of peace-pipe and prayers.
My brother in rock
Must wear warrior guise
Trophy feathers in hair.

Now you will ask me,
"Make feathers from stone?
How almost impossible!"
Not as hard, I swear,
As showing his eyes sad
As only war makes them.

Elegy for an Empress

In memoriam: Bessie Smith.

They use a microphone for singing now,
Willowy girls whose voices wail,
Splintering, pricking briefly at the heart;
None of them anything but frail
Whispers beside the trumpet of your name.
What was the song you circled in your arms,
Close as a lover or a child?
Nothing belongs to them as it did you;
Borrowed emotion lasts awhile,
Shatters its mask, and limps a little, lame.

Where is the wind that bent tall grasses low,
The star that blazed to dim the moon?
Where is the shadow shortened by the sun,
Blotted eternally at noon?
You are remembered. Nothing is the same.

Sonnet on Becoming a Woman of a Certain Age

Above all else, no wish to generate
Much sympathy, nor yet to venerate
A woman who attained this age and wept
For youth that vanished even as she slept;
For her straight back and for a steady pace,
For her smooth brow, for her untroubled face.
Are not these trophies salvaged from the years
Enough to make her scornful of hot tears?
The global villages have children lost
That she could save, and reckon not the cost.
In India, a woman of her own age
Should earn respect, be sought out as a sage.

A Jar of Jelly Beans

For William Carlos Williams.

You, good doctor, probably kept
A fat jar of jelly beans for your
Reluctant small patients, noting
For your own pleasure how sun
Made stained glass of the contents.

You knew you had to hurt to help
Sometimes, and offered sweetness
As solace for heroic achievement:
"See, I didn't cry; but I wanted to…"
You understood the stoicism there.

At the end of a bittersweet day,
When children of the poor lasted
Another twenty-four hours in spite
Of the worst prognosis, you smiled
Tiredly, and reached for a jelly bean.

Souvenir

The kid is a redhead
Norman Rockwell would
Have loved: milk-white
Skin turning painfully
Red under searing sun,
There in the bleachers
He can feel his bones
Bleaching. Thirsty
Again, he counts his
Pocket change. Vendors
Sing siren songs of
Twelve-ounce drinks
Frosty and beaded
With cool condensation.
But no, he's spent too
Much on the souvenir
Program—since it's full
Of hero-photos, that's
Not too much at all.
The heat dazzles, sucking
Energy like marrow from
His bones. He's tired.
Oh, never tireder than now.
But then! Crack of ball
Against bat and there it
Goes! Up and up and UP,
Blurred by trajectory,
Like a bird ascending the
Blue dome of sky. He can
Let his heart soar with
The homerun ball. All
This is happening on a
Mid-Summer day, souvenir
To be remembered for
A long lifetime after.

The Hat

She put on happiness
Like a hat – forgotten
And shelved for years.
A wisp of a smile beguiled her
Face; she tilted her chin up like
A sunflower, expecting sun *and* rain.

Garrick Ohlsson Plays Rachmaninoff

Boettcher Concert Hall, Denver, 1982

The pianist, like some young athlete,
Helmeted and ready for the game,
Appears in this arena garbed
In faultless black and white
(Roars from the crowd),
Approaches the Leviathan he is full
Of force to tame. He knows the number
Of his enemy is only eighty-eight.
And he draws disciplining breath,
And comes in on the beat from beckoning
Baton. He has an army of a hundred
Players to blazon all his colors on.

Some of his army are, like Joan of Arc,
Frail women in a soldier's guise;
These frail vessels draw their bows
Full true and venerate no legends of
The lesser of the sexes. Once, Amazons
In surreal surprise, surrendered half
Their sex in aiming for perfection's
Goal, their truest love, the very center
Of their arrows, and, not arrogant at all,
They bowed as now their sisters
Make their violins and cellos sing,
And wend their sweet, romantic
Antic way along Sergei Vassillevich's road.

Back to the main event: when Garrick Ohlsson
Plays, the very firmament shall ring. With
Perfect arches of arpeggios, he builds cathedrals
Out of air, and all bowed heads in this great
Hall are met in adoration there.

A Little Night Music

For Mary, on her last journey.

Let there be Mozart playing when she leaves;
May all his lightsome joy beguile her heart,
Remembering all the picnics in the park,
And every garden she had ever made;
The taste of just-ripe plums be savored now,
And half a bottle of good wine be shared;
Let all this be comforting at the last.

She does not need us anymore, you know;
That is the hardest thing to reconcile
For all of us she has to leave behind.
And yesterday, when we were young, we thought
This day would never come, but we were wrong.
Let *Eine Kleine Nachtmusik* reprise
And ease her passage into blessed night.

Stepping Out of the Frame

Thomas Gainsborough's The Blue Boy.

His name was Jonathan...
When Sir Thomas painted
His round and rosy face,
He was just a boy waiting
To shed the blue he posed in.
Satin was bad enough; lace
Was, if possible, even worse:
It felt scratchy on his skin.

But, worst of all, the costume
Was a century older than he.
Knee britches and silk hose,
For goodness sake! He felt
Absurd; his cheeks flamed.
(The painter's eye delighted:
All the better for the blushes.)

Oh, and we must not forget
The hat he would not put on,
Could not be coaxed to wear.
It even bore a dashing feather.

The painter, his father's friend,
Took mere merchant's son and
Dressed him in cerulean satin
For the image of aristocracy.

Young Jonathan held no illusions,
He could hardly wait to escape
The prison of the studio and wear
His everyday
And then go out to play.

Discovery

When I was very young, heedless then
As dandelion fluff blown by the wind,
My mother's voice was always in the air,
Stirring me from daydreams, shifting my
Focus from self to others, exacting action
I was slow to take her placid, deliberate
Child. I was quick enough to do things
The wrong way because it was more fun,
And I shut out her voice whenever I could.

But now, since she is so long gone, I harvest
Whatever of her perennials still turn up
In my secret garden of memory, arranging
Them carefully, their colors astonishingly
Still bright and vital, still nurturing my needs.

Notes on a River Called Time

Midstream, this suddenly narrowed river.
Here only a little, dappled brook,
Surprisingly seems not to go on forever,
Over glistening shoals of golden sand
As when we were ridiculously young.
Enter an endless perspective:
We are among sunlit shadows, bright and dark,
And here a smooth pool invites our reflective
– Not vain, but thoughtful – look.
Do we now ever gratefully recall
A certain, green-gold summer's day?
Do we remember the strength and pull
Of one who swam these waters far better
Than we thought we could, urging us on and on?
Midstream is the time for catching breath
And taking stock, and much, much less of talk.
Let's take *one* more dive! Say, "Yes" – it's fun.
Water carries voices down stream, calling us Home.
You'd better hurry, though – it's getting late.

Afternotes

Index of Titles

Index of Titles (continued)

Index of First Lines

Index of First Lines (continued)

Index of First Lines (continued)

Acknowledgments

I owe thanks to so many generous people who gave this book that most valued of all gifts, time. Mentioned or not, I appreciate their attention to the most minute details, since "trifles make perfection, but perfection is no trifle."

Many people read the manuscript in its various stages from seedling to flower, and added their input as an eagle-eyed editor or just with a judicious look. Most notably, these include Maggie Giza, Bob Pugel, Ph.D., Ann Klaiman, Sue Ann Elkins, Gwen Scott, Carolee Asia, Kenn Amdahl, Betty Jane Hill, Loretta Ludlum Taylor, Nancy Finan Davis, and Pat Freiburghaus, who along with her husband Kurt are the best neighbors a writer could hope for.

I am truly grateful for the tutelage of Mary Elizabeth Crawford Joines, which meant more to me than any college class; the support of my readers and critique group near and far, including Nancy Hegan, Trina Lambert, Mary Oliver, Ida Freilinger, Rebecca Burroughs, and Lorna Kelly; and for the inspiration of all my church friends and pastors, Vernon Kurz, Charles Wright, Thomas Hall, John Gaudreau, and the women's guild of Salem United Church.

My poetry has been formed by five generations of family, many of whom appear in this book: my parents Harold and Ida Norman Davis; my brother and friend, Warren "Brud" Davis; and cousins Keith Thompson, Arline Jones Hendricks, Mary Grow, and niece and nephews Jeff, Bob, John and Tricia Davis and their families. Finally, without my daughter Betsy, her husband Elon and my three grandchildren, Clary, Odessa and Leo, there would be far less poetry in my world.

Thank you, Rocky Mountain Women's Institute, for setting me free to write; Poetry Society of Colorado for the encouragement that accompanies awards; and for the Denver Branch, of The National League of American Pen Women, for feedback that collectively encouraged the book's progress; additionally, National Writers' Association for two significant national awards that gave me confidence when I most needed it.

About the Author

Jane Davis Carpenter's award-winning poems have appeared in *The New York Times, The Bloomsbury Review, Good House-keeping, Woman's Day, ByLine, Evergreen Living, Snapshots* and *Sightings.* Her work has also been chosen by literary magazines such as *Pandora* and *Salomé*, published in her hometown newspaper The Denver Post, and selected for juried collections such as *Golden Harvest* and The National League of American Pen Women's *Collage.*

A frequent speaker and workshops leader, Jane has presented her work to television, radio and live audiences in a variety of popular, professional and academic venues. She is an active member of Colorado Pen Women and other professional and cultural organizations. Her previous books include *Art Nouveau Dreams* and four other collections of her poetry.

Jane's first job was as a New York Times copy-girl while attending college. She went on to work as a reporter for other newspapers before earning her B.A. *magna cum laude* from Syracuse University. Born in New Jersey, Jane earned her first dollar from the Newark Sunday Call, which published a poem she submitted at age 8.

About the Book Designer

Seattle artist Liz Gasper is delighted to be the designer of this book and its companion websites; JaneDavisCarpenter.com and PoetryPoetryPoetry.com. Her career has embraced public and community art, visual design and educational endeavors for institutions throughout the Pacific Northwest and Alaska.

A former Fellow at the National Endowment for the Arts in Washington, DC, she earned her B.A. in Studio Art from Linfield College in Oregon and a certificate in Desktop Publishing for Print and Web from Bellevue College.

Colophon

This advance edition of What to Make of Silence was created using Adobe InDesign CS4, and Microsoft Word and printed using on demand technology. The type families used in this book are Century Gothic and Nueva.

The cover illustration shows wildflowers blooming on the slopes of a quiet valley in the Rocky Mountains near Denver, Colorado. The cover illustration is based on a photograph taken in August, 2008: 1/25sec at f/22, 34mm on a zoom lens in a Nikon D300. Further effects and enhancements were created in Photoshop CS4.

Contact

For more information about Jane Davis Carpenter and Liz Gasper, as well as information on readings, signings and workshops on poetry, book design, and internet-based publishing, please visit:

PoetryPoetryPoetry.com

JaneDavisCarpenter.com